SAFER THAN A KNOWN WAY

SAFER THAN A KNOWN WAY

An Escape Story of World War II

Philip Newman

WILLIAM KIMBER · LONDON

First published in 1983 by
WILLIAM KIMBER & CO. LIMITED
100 Jermyn Street
London, SW1Y 6EE

ISBN 0-7183-0419-5

Typeset by Jubal Multiwrite Limited
and printed and bound in Great Britain by
The Garden City Press Limited,
Letchworth, Hertfordshire, SG6 1JS

I said to the man who stood at the gate
of the year –
'Give me a light that I may tread safely
into the unknown.'
And he replied
'Go out into the darkness and put your
hand into the hand of God.
That shall be to you better than light and
safer than a known way.'

Quoted by HM King George VI in
his Christmas broadcast 1939 from
'God Knows' by Minnie Louise
Haskins.

Contents

List of Illustrations

List of Maps

An Appreciation

This book is the fulfilment of a promise I made to myself some forty years ago.

Among many experiences during the evacuation through Dunkirk and subsequent prisoner-of-war life, my vow concerns one so vivid in reflection that the passing of the years can do nothing to dull it.

Since the end of the war medical commitments have claimed a disproportionate amount of my time and the opportunity to set down the story never arose. But now in retirement an attempt has been made to discharge my personal obligation in giving an account of what happened and to record the events leading up to the occasion and the great benefit which I derived from it.

It is my deepest wish to dedicate this book to Bernard Pigeon and to Lucie, his charming wife, for their outstanding courage and sagacity, who, together with their fellow patriots, gave so selflessly and at such great risk to themselves.

In writing this book I want to express my everlasting gratitude to Barbara Clayton for all that she has done in typing illegible long-hand and in correcting and editing the text, and to my wife, Anne, for her constant encouragement and for freeing my time from many other things that should have been done.

Acknowledgements

I wish to express my gratitude to Baroness Airey of Abingdon, to Mrs Peggy Langley, to Mrs P.S. Finlayson and to *Le Journal Liberté Dimanche de Rouen* for kindly supplying photographs, to Anthony Sheil Associates for permission to quote from 'God Knows', a verse from *The Gate of the Year* by Minnie Louise Haskins published by Hodder & Stoughton, and to the Rouen Public Archives for access to their photographic collection.

CHAPTER ONE

The Wounded of Dunkirk

At five minutes to two on Friday, 1st September 1939, the house surgeon, Bernard Lucas, and I were waiting in the entrance hall of The Middlesex Hospital for our chief, Mr Blundell Bankart, to arrive. He had a reputation for meticulous punctuality. Always on a Friday he was met by his staff at 2.0 p.m. sharp and after a hasty greeting would proceed forthwith, walking at a fast pace, to visit his wards and many other patients in different parts of the hospital, but this Friday was a little different.

Poland had been invaded early that morning and the United Kingdom was virtually at war with Germany.

As the three of us stood there discussing the ominous situation a figure came rapidly to join us. It was another Middlesex surgeon, Somerville Hastings. Apart from his distinction as an otolaryngologist he was noted for his political motivation which was inclined to the left. At that time he was Chairman of the Hospitals and Medical Services Committee and later Chairman of the London County Council. He took Bankart by the hand and with excited eyes fixed his attention, saying:

'We have got today something we have been chasing for twenty years, a National Hospital Service.'

It had been forecast by some, should war come, that there could be ten thousand casualties during the first night. The creation of an Emergency Medical Service appealed as an essential answer to a potentially disastrous situation. Our colleague was elated, but few then realised that it was the harbinger of the National Health Service.

After the round we were invited by Sister Kirchin to have tea and there we discussed the implications of the crisis as it would affect patients and staff. Very soon it became obvious that we knew practically nothing about plans for the future. Bankart then took us down to the office of the Secretary Superintendent. It was indeed a nucleus of activity and we learned that all patients would be evacuated to outlying hospitals as soon as possible and that staff continuing with the Hospital Service (The Emergency Medical Service) would be allocated to one of those areas. On the other hand those destined to be called up for the armed services in the near future would become redundant.

The War Office, foreseeing the need for specialists in addition to general duty medical officers, had invited junior specialists to join a list of a supplementary reserve of officers, to be called up in the event of war.

I had already volunteered and so knew that my destiny lay with the Army.

After a few weeks I was ordered to report to the Barracks at Crookham for preliminary training and later was posted as a surgical specialist to the 12th Casualty Clearing Station at Stockgrove Park, near Leighton Buzzard. After a few hours there it became manifest that this unit was in a state of formation from raw personnel.

It was indeed fortunate for the unit that Colonel Cantlie (later Lieutenant-General Sir Neil Cantlie) was its creator. His full complement would consist of twelve officers and over a hundred other ranks. As the numbers built up it became clear that very few had any previous military experience. The officers' mess, to consist of two specialists, four general duty doctors, three padres, a dental surgeon and a quartermaster, were, with the exception of the latter, raw recruits. The majority of the other ranks, so called nursing orderlies, were rural workers, many from Shropshire.

It was the task of our Commanding Officer to mould us into an efficient, mobile, military hospital. He undoubtedly had the necessary qualities, extensive military and medical experience, teaching ability and a persuasive sense of humour.

After the day's work was over it was apparent that he looked forward to a jovial evening in the Mess, but maybe the standard of social intercourse that we Service new boys achieved did not add up. On the third night that most of us had been there for dinner he indicated that he was not feeling at his best and retired prematurely before the coffee. In his absence a few sympathetic remarks were made about our Chief and duodenal ulcer was mentioned during the conversation, but none of us knew him personally and he had spoken very little about his health.

With the coffee we moved to more comfortable chairs and pushed them into groups round the Quartermaster, from whom we had much to learn. Topper Brown was very keen to impress us that everything was not always available from his stores.

'Over the other side', he said, 'you may only get a Soldier's Supper.'

'What is that,' I asked.

'A piss and get into bed,' was his reply.

That gave us a laugh and shut us up for a bit. Then suddenly we turned round because the door at the end had been pushed open and in came an odd figure. He was dressed in a cloth cap, old trousers and a long-sleeved sweater. He had a dirty face and started to play a flute held in his right hand. The left sleeve was empty. It appeared that he had no arm until a curled finger projecting through his flies from within was spotted, holding an old enamel mug. This would-be entertainer approached the group of chairs rattling the mug and we all instinctively felt for our pockets. It was our Colonel. He brought the house down and undoubtedly made our Mess a happier place to spend an evening. Unfortunately for us he was promoted to higher things when we left the country to join the British Expeditionary Force but his image remained always in our Mess and his 'fluting' was undoubtedly a stimulus for many hilarious evenings.

The unit landed in France on 1st February to spend three and a half months idling in the so-called phoney war.

Some three weeks before the balloon went up on 10th May the unit had been moved to the Béthune area and ordered to open up on the sports ground at Annezin. There had been plenty of time for preparation when very little was happening in the locality. Then suddenly casualties had started to pour in from an army that had been fighting and retreating and fighting and retreating for seven days. Many were so bad after such rugged transport and lack of proper treatment that they must have hoped to have reached their final resting place. Nurses and orderlies had worked day and night to do what they could to resuscitate and succour the wounded, three surgical teams had operated continuously and the administration had fought to keep supplies going and to get or beg transport for the evacuation of the patients. Safe transfer back to a base hospital was their main concern.

In static warfare it was the routine function of a Casualty Clearing Station to accept injured and sick, to carry out emergency and immediately necessary treatment and evacuate to a general hospital, but there in Béthune it was a nightmare to know what to do.

The line of evacuation south and west had been cut by the formidable left hook of the German Panzer Corps advancing from the breakthrough at Namur to the Channel ports. To the east and north were the fighting fronts and the only possible way out was to the north-west in the direction of Dunkirk.

After five days of full activity when the very seams of the marquees were bursting with wounded the unit had been ordered to close and then within a few hours there had come a counter order 'It is vital that you remain open.' By then the sports ground was being strafed from the air and shelled from the land and it had soon become obvious that our unit was away out beyond the front line projecting into no man's land of a very fluid stability.

At dawn a staff officer had arrived with an order to close and get out within half an hour. He was followed by a stream of ambulances and lorries. Within a very short time two hundred and fifty wounded, some walking but mostly stretcher cases, were loaded on to the ambulances and were away. Essential medical equipment and supplies were thrown on to the lorries, the marquees were slashed and the grand-stands, which contained the bulk of equipment, were set on fire. The whole unit was away within the hour and as it left a low flying aircraft dropped a stick of bombs among the tents to complete the process of demolition.

The convoy of lorries, independent of the ambulances with the wounded which had gone on ahead, had made its way north through Hinges so as to avoid the congestion of evacuees on the main roads. It was fortunate to find a bridge over the Canal d'Aire still intact and as it passed over, troops on the other side were seen to be busy camouflaging their tanks and digging hard in an attempt to hold yet another of many front lines.

Who, a fortnight earlier, in their wildest dreams, could have thought that Béthune would have to be defended, and of all directions, from the south?

Once over the Canal the convoy filtered slowly north through the Belgian border to Poperinge. Here our Commanding Officer, Colonel Pank, received instructions to proceed ten kilometres along the Dunkirk road to Proven where he was to await further orders. No sooner had the unit arrived at this little town than the Commanding Officer virtually gave the order to dismiss and everyone without further thought quite naturally fell asleep in the lorries or by the road side. The next day had been one of recuperation and stock taking of what little there was left and drivers and NCOs were sent out to replenish stores, dressings, beds and any other equipment which would help the unit to open again as a fully going concern. It was a matter of hunting around because there were units with surplus stock which were liable to be moved back at any moment.

Sunday the 26th dawned bright and clear. No new orders had come in so the Commanding Officer asked the Church of England Chaplain to hold a service in the open. It was after the service that Colonel Pank, Major Longridge and I decided to go for a walk before lunch. Conversation was not abundant. A gentle country stroll in the warm sun was joy enough while our mental reserves were finding replenishment for what was to come. Although we knew little of the overall picture it needed no imagination to realise that the whole BEF was now surrounded except for a rapidly diminishing base on the coast. It stuck out like a sore thumb into the holocaust of overwhelming odds with ever increasing tension and congestion within its confines and now that Calais had fallen there was only one port remaining to this elongated bridgehead, Dunkirk.

We did not know that during the Church service a telegram from the Secretary of State, Anthony Eden, had been handed to General Gort at his Headquarters not far away. It announced the fading hope of a relieving counter attack to or from the Somme in the south, in which case the safety of the BEF became of primary importance. It mentioned evacuation from the beaches

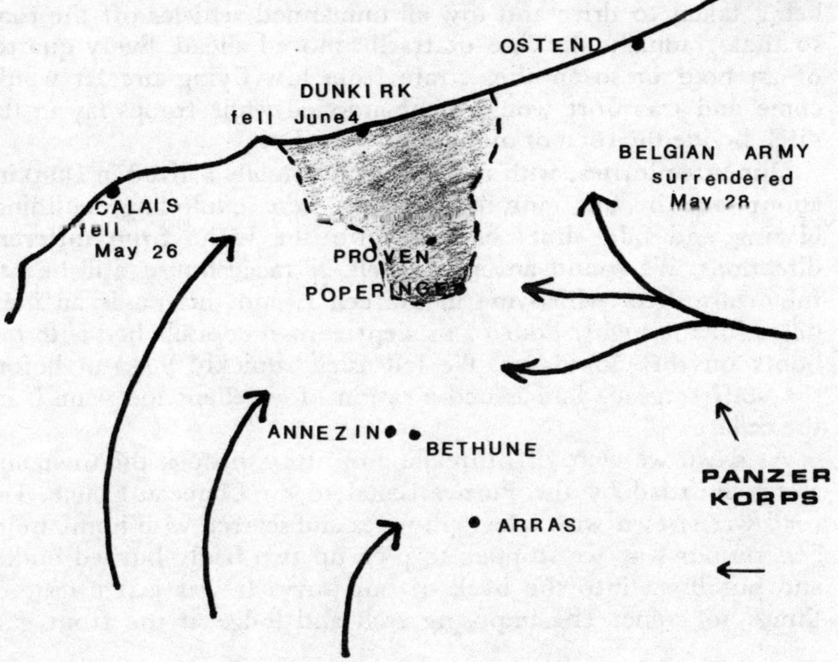

assisted by the Royal Navy and RAF. Things got moving quickly and as we arrived back at the Unit we noticed a dispatch rider. The message was handed to Colonel Pank. It was an order to proceed to Dunkirk forthwith and open up at the Chapeau-Rouge, Rosendael.

The officers and senior NCOs were assembled and the order read out. The unit for transport purposes was split into three parties each to travel independently to Chapeau-Rouge. It was a distance of about thirty kilometres and we estimated a maximum of two hours so that there should be time in the evening for opening up, but little did we know.

I was given charge of Party 2 and we left during the afternoon, but many other units had been ordered to proceed to Dunkirk and the roads became increasingly impossible; refugees, cattle, broken down and bombed and strafed vehicles became an impossible obstacle as we got within ten kilometres of our destination. Hoping to hurry things up we turned north on to a quieter road but were discouraged by reports of an armoured division approaching from the north. It soon became obvious that we had to cross the Canal at Bergues and that this meant turning back and getting on to the main road again. The state of the road near Bergues had become so bad that drastic action was being taken to drive and tow all unmanned vehicles off the road so that gradually the line of traffic moved ahead. Every quarter of an hour or so another strafe from low flying aircraft would come and transport would be abandoned while troops lay in the ditch beside the road or under their vehicles.

Our three lorries, with forty men, eventually arrived in Dunkirk about one in the morning. Bombs were exploding, buildings blazing and odd shots cracked into the night from different directions. We found an empty, tall, terraced house, still beautifully furnished, with wine in the cellar, and this made an ideal billet for the night. Four of us slept across a double bed with our boots on the eiderdown. We fell asleep quickly but not before the staff sergeant had issued a ration of excellent red wine from the cellar.

At dawn we were off, threading our way through the town and along the road by the Furnes Canal to the Chapeau-Rouge. The road was strewn with telegraph wires and scarred with bomb holes and on our way we stopped to pick up two badly burned bodies and put them into the back of our lorry. It was just a taste of things to come. The imposing arch and lodge at the front gate was close to the bridge over the Canal. The Chapeau-Rouge was a large modern red brick château with a central tower, standing in a park of some three or four acres. There was a line of out-houses and a kitchen garden. The main part of the park was open grass with a large ornamental pond. On the other side near the Canal was a cluster of marquees and tents displaying a large red cross. It was a French field ambulance unit.

The first party had already arrived and had got moving with beds and stores, but there was an awful languid feeling among all of us in having to open up again and hold the baby while everyone else was running for home. I reported to the Commanding Officer and was told to select a site for an operating theatre. A room facing the park with large windows on the ground floor gave ready access to the rest of the building, good lighting and easy parking for the x-ray van outside to provide not only portable x-rays but current for emergency lighting, should the house supply fail. Within an hour two teams were ready to start operating so adept had we become at opening up and closing down at short notice.

It was none too early. Ambulances were already arriving in great numbers packing the drive and the lawns. Sorting the cases, an

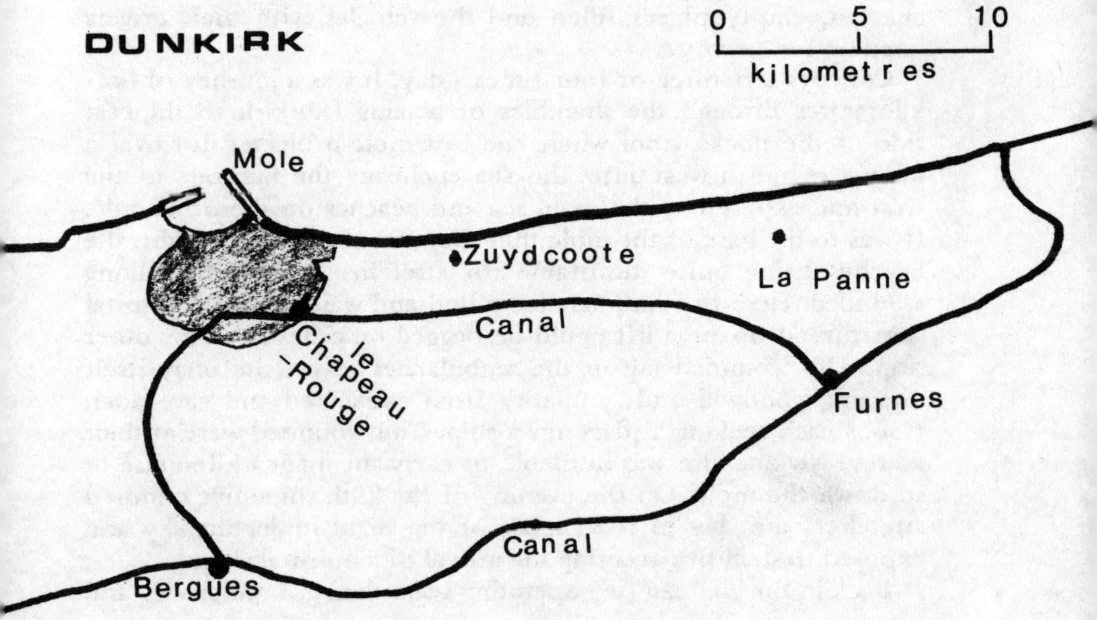

activity commonly known as triage, for type and priority of treatment and disposal was a key job of major importance in an active casualty clearing unit. We were fortunate in having two experts of very suitable temperament. Gordon was a Highlander from Aberdeenshire whom everybody loved and Herbert an Irishman with a flourishing practice in Woking. Both were extroverts and complementary to each other, giving an undoubted boost to the morale of patients and staff while mindful of their task of exacting difficulty. Cases requiring surgery were kept nearby so as to avoid transport up and down stairs and those too ill for any active treatment requiring shelter, rest and any resuscitation available were put into the largest room on the ground floor. Most of the wounded were fit enough for evacuation home and they were returned to the ambulances which were lined up for convoy to the docks.

As the word got around that the 12th CCS was open in Dunkirk wounded poured in not only from the retreating forces but from local bombardment and shelling from the strafed troops massing on the beaches and from the ships which were intermittently dive-bombed by Stukas and machine gunned and bombed by low flying aircraft. The park soon became a scene of great activity, a rallying point where ambulances could be inspected, their dead removed, the very ill and those requiring surgery transferred to the château, empty places filled and the vehicles with their drivers lined up for convoy.

Convoys left three or four times a day. It was a journey of four kilometres through the shambles of blazing Dunkirk to the east side of the docks from where the east mole projected for over a kilometre north-west into the sea enclosing the harbour to the west and exposed to the open sea and beaches on the other side. It was to the base of the mole that the wounded were brought, the beaches being quite unsuitable for stretcher cases and walking wounded. Here the ambulances waited and waited until a hospital ship turned up or a lift could be begged on a destroyer or other ship. The wounded lay in the ambulances or on the quay itself awaiting goodwill and sympathy from exhausted and care-laden troops each seeking a place on a ship. The wounded were at their mercy. No one else was available to carry them for a kilometre or so down the mole. On the evening of the 29th some five hundred stretcher cases lay in rows most of the night under the sky and exposed to shell fire awaiting the arrival of a hospital ship.

Back in the château two operating teams had got under way and there is little need to qualify the depressing nature of the surgeon's job. Some wounded had been in the ambulances for many hours or even days and water and nourishment was their main need but with all goodwill and little wisdom tourniquets had been applied for severe haemorrhage with a view to surgery within two hours and this had never become available. Gangrenous limbs had to be removed and ever since then the idea of a tourniquet has been to me an anathema. Perforating wounds of the abdomen, wounds bubbling with gas gangrene and those containing large foreign bodies were priorities for surgery and fractures had to be splinted in preparation for transport. Those were the days before antibiotics: How different was the whole aspect of war surgery; the fear of infection dominated the surgeon's objective and the smell of the wounds was unforgettable.

Two surgeons, one anaesthetist and four theatre orderlies made up the two teams with the anaesthetist, Tim McCoy, responsible for both tables. Two of the orderlies looked after the instruments and sutures and the other two transported patients in and out and were responsible for all the back-stage duties. Our eight sisters had left us in Annezin and we hoped had got safely home but we missed them very much. Operating went on during the 27th, 28th and 29th, day and night, with short intervals for refreshment and a little sleep. The officers' baggage had been put in a little room next to the theatre and this became our mess where we slept on top of the baggage and were provided with bully beef, biscuits and whisky.

Conditions deteriorated daily. The Germans had got up to the Bergues Canal and could reach us with their shells. There was a French battery either side of our compound and these were frequently dive bombed by Stukas. Such attacks created a lot of noise and shaking but did not deter the gunners from persistent retaliating activity. More and more our park became filled with ambulances and walking casualties. On 29th May, two paddle steamers, the *Fenella* and the *Crested Eagle* were moored at the end of the mole. The *Fenella* was hit with seven hundred men and wounded aboard and was abandoned and the troops transferred to the *Crested Eagle*. After casting off she was dive bombed and set on fire. Many were badly burned, some killed and some drowned. Others came ashore and were brought up to Rosendael in lorries. Those too feeble to stand lay down but others wandered about the grounds in and out of the shrubberies, burned and half naked seeking shade from the hot sun and distraction from their suffering. In the dressing room of the château their burns were cleaned and sprayed with tannic acid, a treatment very much in vogue at that time. It had come from China where burns had been treated for thousands of years with strong infusions of tea.

The château soon became full and the grounds took over as an open ward for the wounded and the dying. Getting drink and food, administering first aid and the basic essentials of nursing and burying the dead was about as much as the harassed unit could manage. Very soon it became obvious that evacuation was the only worthwhile service for the wounded. To stay in Rosendael meant certain capture. It was under shell fire and had less and less to offer as a hospital where food, medical supplies, clothing and shelter were fast running out.

That night at 22.00 hours an order came through. All wounded were to be put into vehicles, driven to the docks and the unit was to go home. The reaction was electric. All vehicles in the neighbourhood were collected and lined up in the drive from the château to the main gate. The walking cases were packed into lorries and everyone worked relentlessly to get the stretcher cases out of the château and into the ambulances. We were to learn that the hospital carrier *Dinard* was on its way and due to dock during the night. Her master reported the difficulty of making contact with those in charge of the wounded and of the continual bursting of shells and bombs as she lay alongside the mole. Some of our wounded got aboard but by midnight, with the tide ebbing, she left with only a foot of water to spare.

By 04.00 hours there was a counter order that the evacuation had ended and the unit was to remain open. It would be hard to describe the despair and despondency of the wounded and the unit as stretchers were carried back to the château which they had left six hours previously with orders to go home. Wounded and fit men alike escaped into temporary sleep where they lay.

By dawn fresh convoys of wounded were arriving and the theatre was reopened for essential surgery but the overall value that a team of seven could give by keeping two operating tables going eventually subsided into significance in comparison with helping with evacuation. One wounded man put aboard a ship for home surpassed in value almost anything that could be done in the operating theatre. By 30th May most of the officers with drivers and orderlies were involved in loading and driving ambulances to the docks, unloading and begging a lift for each stretcher case from the flocks of demoralised soldiers passing down the mole. It was the only way. A ship might dock half a mile down the mole which was packed with anxious men all waiting to get on board. Transporting wounded, unless a hospital carrier was in, became an increasing challenge.

The mole was controlled by Captain Tennant, in charge of naval services, and Brigadier Parminter, in charge of military evacuation. Captain Tennant had beside him an AB with a flash lamp. They stood there watching a ship or ships cruising at high speed in zig-zag fashion outside and at the appropriate moment the Captain would say 'Bring in the 'so and so' '. A few flashes from the lamp and in would come the ship. Troops packing the mole and standing there queueing hour after hour under shell fire were not slow to get aboard and the ship could be away in ten to fifteen minutes. A stretcher had to be there in the right place at the appropriate moment with dedicated volunteer carriers to stand a chance of getting aboard. Manning the stretchers was a soul-searing business eliciting no sympathy or encouragement either from the Captain or from the Brigadier, but yet no definite refusal. They knew full well that a stretcher took far longer to be put on board and occupied a space where six or eight men could stand. Hospital carriers were for the wounded and medical personnel and ships were for the troops and Britain desperately needed every fit man that she could get.

By dawn on 1st June conditions had become so bad that we decided to close the theatre permanently and the Commanding Officer sent Munro, an officer of a civilian Red Cross unit, and myself off to scour the town for other hospital accommodation.

We visited two civilian hospitals but of course they were inundated with civilian casualties and not surprisingly could offer no help. During the night, at the second hospital that we tried, there had been a bomb in the children's ward and the nuns told us all about it. Relentlessly they had worked through the night, treating the casualties and clearing up the mess but their attitude was unforgettable; one of complete objectivity and factual assessment, no panic nor emotional out-flow, a quiet, cool acceptance of the inevitable, and a fundamental confidence whether injury, rape or death be their lot, that things were going according to plan and the Almighty knew his job. It was my first experience of nuns under potentially panic conditions and it made a deep impression. Their composure and physical and mental grace came as a moral transfusion and helped me to realise that there was reason for and something much bigger that transcended the horrors of war. Here was faith in the most impressive form that I had ever encountered. We thanked them and bade farewell and left the hospital morally refreshed.

Outside we pulled up the truck so as to discuss quietly our next move but with lighted cigarettes we sat in silence picturing the British and French armies fleeing through Dunkirk and those grand ladies standing their ground and doing their job regardless of the consequences. It was the first time for many days that either of us had had time to think.

There was little left but to return to the Unit and give the Commanding Officer our negative report.

On arriving at the château it soon became obvious that things were deteriorating. A shell had exploded in the rear corner of the building and others had landed in the grounds among the wounded. Fortunately a convoy had left during the morning with about a hundred stretcher cases. But something else was in the air and this we learnt from the Commanding Officer. The Deputy Director of Medical Services, 1st Corps, had called and ordered the unit to evacuate that evening at 20.00 hours, leaving one medical officer and ten other ranks for every hundred wounded. This was refreshing news for us all, never really thinking that there was any chance of getting away as the Germans had been expected at any time since the fall of Calais nearly a week ago. It had been decided that there would be a ballot. A count of the wounded at midday had made a sum of two hundred and thirty and so it seemed that three medical officers and thirty men would be needed to stay. We heard that the ballot was to be at 14.00 hours, one for the seventeen medical officers now in the mess and another for the one hundred and twenty or so other ranks. Every name was to go into the hat and be drawn out on the principle that first out was first to go.

It was a tense moment as we assembled in the now disused operating theatre. Lissy, the Church of England padre, had been asked to draw for the men and Cockie, the Roman Catholic padre, for the officers.

An account of the draw featured in the unit diary and an extract was reported in the official history of the Army Medical Services published by the Stationery Office in 1956.

> A ballot was accordingly carried out for both officers and men at 14.00 hours, on the principle first out of the hat first to go and last out of the hat last to go. There were some seventeen

officers working at the CCS exclusive of padres, etc. and it was as tense and dramatic a draw as any in which one could wish to partake; there were some two hundred and thirty casualties remaining at the time and the last three named were those of an officer who had got separated from his field ambulance and joined us at Béthune, another who had been sent over for beach duties at Dunkirk and had only been in France for a few days, and the surgical specialist.

I shall not forget the secret agony as the names were read out, twelve so and so, thirteen so and so, and still my name had not come forward. Fourteen, fifteen, sixteen and seventeen were Herbert, Hewer, Williamson and Newman. As to whether three or four would stay depended on the count at the time of departure but at least I knew my fate.

It was certain capture. The only glimmer of hope lay in the possible evacuation of all the wounded, which at that moment seemed remote but later in the day an order came in that departure of the unit should be delayed as there was news of a hospital ship.

The afternoon dragged on comparatively quietly and only a moderate number of new wounded arrived. We awaited news of the sighting of a hospital ship, in which case everyone would at once spring into action loading the stretcher cases into ambulances and the walking wounded into lorries. Many were busy lining up the available vehicles and scouting the town for more, but drivers to the mole were apt to disappear and that was where much of the transport remained, causing great obstruction to new convoys arriving.

By the early evening there was still no news of a hospital ship and final orders for the departing unit had not been given. There was no great urge to load the wounded in anticipation as we had done the night before last. The wear and tear, should nothing result, both physically and mentally, for the patients and personnel was far too devastating.

In the lull there was a spontaneous wish on the part of the padres and those fated to remain to hold a service of farewell. Perhaps they wanted to attempt to bridge the gap between the good and bad fortune and to offer a prayer for the survival of all those destined to stay. We climbed the many stairs to the top room of the tower where no wounded were, and stood there in a bewildered bunch. Lissy created a service of touching moment. It was short and to the point and followed by throttled emotion. The group remained still for a little and gradually dispersed without conversation, conscious that there was nothing to say. Lissy stood by the door and shook everyone warmly by the hand as each filtered down the stairway.

Cockie, our beloved Roman Catholic padre, had been standing in the corner at the back of the room. He came to me, took me by the hand and giving me his Crucifix said, 'This will see you home'. On one occasion I had seen him lay this Cross on the chest of a recently departed patient while giving him the last sacrament. I imagined it was something of inestimable value to him and was overwhelmed that he should give it to me especially at such a time when it was most needed. Sincerity was a rare mood for Cockie but at such moments it dominated his potential joviality.

Everyone loved Cockie. He was the favourite in the officers' mess. He had come from a very strict order into the Services and as a natural camouflage to his lack of interest in worldly affairs he adopted an almost permanent frivolity founded on a vivid turn of Irish humour. He showed no desire to know what money was for as previously he had lived without it. At the end of the month when he received his pay he settled his mess bill and then with the residue in his pockets walked the streets of whatever town it was and gave it away to any deserving person. The coins he kept in his trouser pockets for the children. They soon got to know him and when it was all gone he would turn the linings inside out, indicating that there was none left. He would arrive back at the mess like the Pied Piper with a stream of children behind him.

The count of the wounded in the evening was two hundred and sixty-five and the Commanding Officer gave the final order, as we expected, that three officers and thirty men were to stay. From then on the unit got separated psychologically into two, those to go and those to stay, and each subconsciously avoided the other, the majority packing and lining up and the minority continuing to attend to the multiple needs of the patients. So embarrassing for both did it become that we were thankful when they left. The moment of departure was tempered by some emotional words of congratulation and goodwill from the Commanding Officer and this spontaneously created three cheers for him from the whole unit. Above all they were conscious that he had worked himself to a limit day and night to get the wounded away.

They departed on time and we were left, thirty-three of us, to look after nearly three hundred wounded and the haunting fear of the Germans to come. There was nothing pleasant about the prospect and activity seemed to be the only diversional remedy. It was about all we could do to keep everyone supplied with sufficient to drink and something to eat.

During the night there was an explosion in front of the château. Underneath the imposing front promenade there was a cellar where I had been operating and one adjoining room where the postoperative patients were still housed. The whole promenade had caved in from a shell burst and covered the patients. With the aid of torches, slabs of paving stone were removed and miraculously all but one of the fourteen men beneath were still alive. Just after that was cleared away the French tented field ambulance was hit with a bomb. It was a shambles. The Commanding Officer and five of his men were killed. This was the final straw because he was an experienced officer whom I had taken to and he gave me a reassuring feeling of confidence especially as the French troops were almost certain to dig in along the front of our grounds for the final stand along the Dunkirk-Furnes Canal which ran just outside our boundary.

On returning to the château to our delight we found that Whitehall, our mess orderly, had cleared out a room in the cellar and put four beds and a table in it. The fourth was for an officer from another unit who had volunteeerd to stay, Lieutenant Forsythe, a magnificent thing for him to have done. The accommodation was not something that we could have ordered but presented with a fait accompli it was a delight. Above all it was somewhere where the four of us could sit and talk and formulate some administrative plan out of the chaos.

It was after dawn on Sunday, the 2nd, at about 5.30 a.m. that a unit of Guards marched into the compound. They had withdrawn from the rear-guard action on the Bergues–Furnes Canal that night and were due for evacuation during the following day. Before marching through Dunkirk to the mole they came into our park to shave and clean up. By then there was little else than pond water and spit and polish available but they made the most wonderful impression. The unit left Rosendael marching in order and later when they got to the quay gave eyes right for General Alexander, who turned out from the bastion to take the salute.

Just after they had gone an order came through by dispatch rider. All walking wounded were to go. Hurriedly four lorries were found and we went around shouting, 'All walking wounded to go'. No more was said, leaving the decision to go or not to go to each individual. It was probably the last hope for anyone to get home. It was astounding who attempted to walk, men with fractured femurs, men with holes in their head and wounds in their chest, men with severe burns or large gaping wounds in their back, going to England in nothing but a blanket.

This motley, pathetic, self-selected, band of hope, was helped into the lorries, many of them no more fit to walk than fly but who was to deny a chance of getting home to any one of them? Once they got to the mole more help from other troops might be forthcoming. Doubtless the policy during the last few days, when no hospital ships were arriving, was priority for evacuation of the fit men. This last order may well have been an attempt to restore humanitarian justice. The tail-boards of the lorries were put up and fastened, and away went four loads of determined souls who had decided the risk preferable to capture. We saw them no more but hoped they got back safely.

But what of those who remained, could nothing be done? The pump had run dry and we were down to drinking pond water rations were low and medical supplies had completely gone. Since dawn wounded had continued to pour in from the retreating rear-guard units and by midday there were four hundred and fifty in our compound.

I decided to get into a car and go down to the mole once more to see if there was any sign of a ship or any person in charge to whom to appeal. A Lincoln Zephyr got through the shambles of the streets quickly and safely and arriving at the bastion to my joy I saw a sentry standing outside. I walked in without any trouble and straight into a meeting. Major-General Alexander was sitting in the middle of the group of British and French officers. I was beckoned to sit down and join them. The General, immaculately dressed, sat straight in his chair and quietly answered questions and discussed problems with the collection of officers in various states of agitation and alarm. The effect of his bearing was unforgettable. Among all the potential panic here was a leader, cool, calculating and approachable, to act as a sheet-anchor in a gale, which he did superbly well.

He looked at me and I said:

'Sir, there are four hundred and fifty wounded at Rosendael. We have no medical supplies and very little food left and conditions are bad. All that we can do for them is to try and get them home.'

For a moment he thought, then turned round to another officer and said:

'Wireless for a hospital ship.' To me he said:

'Go back to your unit and prepare the wounded for evacuation. I will send a dispatch rider as soon as a hospital ship is sighted.'

That was that. I had my orders, the best possible thing was being done and the relief was tremendous.

Arriving back at the unit I called together everyone that could be found and described the fortuitous meeting with General Alexander and his prompt action of wirelessing for a hospital ship. Needless to say the effect was dynamic and it was agreed that loading of the ambulances should start all over again. It meant removing the dead and emptying the château of all stretcher cases. The walking wounded had gone earlier that morning. This new and last ray of hope dominated the hell of the previous frustrated attempts and the wounded doubtless would have voted unanimously to withstand the neglect, pain and suffering which transfer would mean for the slightest chance of not being left behind. We waited. Not until the evening did news come through that a hospital ship had left England. A token convoy of five ambulances left immediately, driven by Hewer, Williamson, Gaze, Evans and myself, with thirty-five wounded on board. This was essentially a reconnaissance convoy to leave the wounded on the quayside, to wait until the hospital ship was spotted arriving and then to return with the empty ambulances to reload and lead the whole convoy to the docks.

Gaze, who had more experience of driving through Dunkirk than any of us, led the convoy and brought us through many hazards safely to the area of the mole. There was Captain Tennant and his signaller still in masterly control of the shipping. We learnt that a hospital ship had left Dover some hours ago but had not yet been sighted from Dunkirk. It was possible that she was cruising at low speed or taking a longer unusual course, waiting for dusk before coming into port. This was an explanation for the moment and might well have been the truth but a hospital ship, adequately marked and maintaining right of protection of the Geneva Convention, should arrive in full daylight. Such protection in this campaign had proved useless as the Captain and crew were well aware and it might be that the skipper had abandoned all faith and adopted a plan of precaution. Most other shipping was waiting for the dark, very little was coming in and out at the present time and the file of men down the mole had come to a standstill.

As the light faded the file began to move and ships were signalled in and left as soon as they were full. British troops had got the message and were now filing in from many directions. Down the other side of the mole there was an increasing queue of Frenchmen.

Our apprehension and disappointment were mounting hour by hour but we could only stay put and hang on in the hope that a hospital ship would appear. We kept in close contact with Captain Tennant when it became dark so as to get immediate warning should one be near in which case the wounded would be unloaded and left by the quayside and the empty ambulances raced back to Rosendael.

But no such information came. The wireless message from General Alexander had been passed to a hospital carrier *Worthing*, a Southern Railway steamer lying in the Downs north of Dover. She had left at 12.55 but by 14.30 hours was attacked by twelve enemy aircraft and badly damaged. The visibility was good and she was clearly marked. It was a deliberate attack, flouting the Geneva Convention. Making water she limped back to base. The *Paris*, a hospital carrier of the same line, was ordered to go in her place and left at 16.48 hours, to suffer a similar fate. She was twice bombed by aircraft and had to be abandoned. The *Paris* could have arrived by 20.00 hours and left with all our wounded on board by midnight, but it was not to be.

As we sat there with the wounded in the ambulances amidst the shells and bombs and the shambles of abandoned vehicles and arms, of dead horses and the wind-driven contents of hundreds of abandoned mail bags, the last of the British rearguard troops went past. The previous night, 1st/2nd June, had been allocated priority for the last British evacuation and the night before that for the French. Tonight was primarily for the French after the remaining British rearguard had got away.

We thought of the wounded, and our colleagues back at Rosendael waiting and waiting for our arrival, their only link with hope and survival. By now they must be thinking that we had abandoned them and gone home. It was eight hours since we had left them.

By 22.00 hours our hope was fast fading and we decided to play our last card, to unload all the wounded down at the base of the mole and commandeer or beg carriers from the passing troops. It was hard work, some were taken by French troops filing down the other side of the mole and some by British soldiers and marines. It was a long carry and the men were in a determined hurry, encouraged by the Navy, whose main concern was to get each ship away as quickly as possible. The last two we carried down ourselves and arrived at the first boat on the French side. It was just casting off and it meant almost chucking the stretchers over the taffrail as the stern pulled away from the side of the mole, leaving an ever widening gap of pitch dark sea. Fortunately they were caught by many willing arms and landed to safety.

It was a relief to know that they had gone.

The file of British troops was now thinning out and at the base where the Captain and Brigadier were still in command we were told that the evacuation was coming to an end, also that there was no signal from a hospital ship.

What was there to do but wait and hope? The alternative of returning without news of a hospital ship to the three hundred waiting wounded in the ambulances was annihilation. To return and bring fifty loaded ambulances to this strategic point at the base of the mole would be massacre.

The file of British troops virtually ceased and just before midnight General Alexander, Brigadier Parminter and a few others got into a motor boat and pulled quickly away in a zig-zag course. Captain Tennant and the signaller left their post after signalling a simple message 'BEF evacuated.'. The British army and navy had gone home – we were alone. Gradually the truth engulfed us in a cloak of desolation. The chance of a hospital ship arriving now was negligible and as we stood there in utter despair one fact slowly penetrated the dazed contents of our skulls. There was only one duty left; to return to Rosendael to prove that we had not deserted and to succour the wounded before and after capture. One of us had disappeared. The remaining four got into two ambulances for the journey back. The known way had now become entirely blocked so that we got separated.

Eventually we found the road along the Canal leading east to Furnes which passed the Chapeau-Rouge. To our right two white Very lights suddenly lit up the sky and we knew that the German front line was near. It was just west of Bergues that they had penetrated the French line and were preparing to advance to the Canal. Fortunately we were not shot at but it was an ominous sign for our hospital grounds on the coming day.

With trepidation we passed through the front gate and came on the leading ambulance of the waiting convoy. The boys had done a wonderful job getting three hundred stretchers out of the château, loading and lining up the ambulances for the road but overall frustration and despair had now taken charge of the patients and the orderlies after waiting for seven hours. All hope had been cast aside. Some lay exhausted, asleep on the ground, and others fought hard to answer the calls for 'water' and 'orderly' which penetrated the dark like cries of drowning men. Falling into line we joined the group with a bucket and cup. No water had come through the mains for three days, the well had gone dry and the only available source was the garden lake. It mattered little so long as the wounded got water.

Outside, during the early hours of Monday morning, the two front lines were waiting for dawn. A barrage of naval guns, French field guns and the retaliating German artillery made an unbelievable din. Both sides were softening up for the final attack to come. Just before dawn the French made a brave counter-attack and penetrated to Galghouck but later were thrown back to Teteghem and later still consolidated on a line from the dunes to the bridge outside our front gate and round Dunkirk to the coast again west of the burning petrol depot. Several times we pleaded with the French Commandant not to dig in in our park because the wounded were still either in the ambulances or laid out on the ground. We foresaw them retreating through the park and even hiding in our cellars which would lead to hand grenades and hand to hand fighting. He was responsive to our requests. He had orders to dig in in our park but promised not to use the château as a refuge.

All that day our grounds were under shell fire. Most of the ambulances had been driven round behind the château for shelter until all the available space was exhausted. The château was hit in three places but it mattered little as most of the wounded were out. What happened in the grounds during that day is not recounted but four of our men were allocated to burying the dead. Most of our orderlies were not averse to this activity and preferred it to nursing, the majority having been drafted from farm work only a few months previously.

When the French showed signs of retreating from our park at dusk it became fairly likely that the Germans would come in at dawn. It was the last possible night for the French troops to get away by boat. In the unbelievable shambles capture seemed inevitable and it was a relief to know that without resistance there would not be a battle in our park. Some sort of plan had to be made for the arrival of the Germans.

Gaze, an ambulance driver, who had voluntarily joined our unit of his own free will was in civilian life an East Anglian farmer and estate agent. He had more than average nous and intelligence and was a genius at finding things out and delivering the goods. Only that morning he had discovered another well in the grounds which restored our clean water supply. He spoke some German and so became a very important person. As the French left the front gate building he took up his post there and with a candle and a cut out tin box hung an illuminated red cross on the outside wall.

Jimmy Langley

Chapeau Rouge Dunkirk

Cockie O'Shea and his crucifix

There was one other invaluable asset to our credit, a wounded German pilot officer. He was put with a few others in the front porch of the château, under a great arch that was comparatively safe from bombardment. Naturally he was treated with considerable respect. He was not unintelligent and responded to our advances. We learnt a few German phrases such as '*Rotes Kreutz*' and '*Nicht schiessen.*' A rota of senior NCOs and officers was made so that each would take an hour to watch through the night, sitting in the front porch. They had strict instructions to wake me as soon as German soldiers were sighted in our grounds. I had a clean uniform hanging in the kitchen where after my uneventful watch from 2 to 3 a.m. I dropped to sleep on the stone floor.

Around 6 a.m. I was shaken vigorously and came round gradually to unwelcome consciousness realising that someone was shouting 'The Germans are here'.

There seemed no panic so I put on my clean uniform and walked to the front porch. The grounds were full of German soldiers talking to the wounded. All the softening up propaganda of taking no prisoners, shooting intelligentsia and officers melted spontaneously into the vivid blue sky.

It was a peaceful scene.

No bombs, no guns, no bullets, no planes, no more diving for cover and splitting eardrums, but the bright sunshine highlighted the agony and devastation of total war. Enacted before our eyes was the background horror and the spontaneous reaction of sympathy and friendship. The conquering troops were already bringing hot soup to the wounded and producing photographs out of well-squashed wallets. A few were engaged in conversation with the German pilot who undoubtedly had spoken in our favour. I stood there in the porch watching the scene and waiting to be beckoned by a German officer but none seemed to be around. I could hear the golden oriole singing in the top of the oak tree close to the château, where I had heard him at odd times before when the racket of warfare had temporarily ceased. This was his day. He could sing to his heart's content, marvelling at the change of scene on the stage beneath him. He had stayed with us through it all. He deserved, like Captain Forsyth and Private Gaze to be made an emeritus fellow of the 12th CCS.

The rest of our stay in Dunkirk as far as we were concerned was a gradual descent from the peak of carnage and destruction to some recognisable form of humanitarian order.

The German pilot officer was taken away at an early stage and maybe as a result of what he passed on we were left practically on our own as a unit. A field battery with some fine horses and guns came through the front gate with the intention of camping down in our park. The officer in charge bade me walk round with him to demonstrate the extent of the grounds. Our communications consisted almost entirely of waving of arms and pointing as neither of us had the desire or the ability to speak the other's language. Above all he was very proud of his horse, which was a fine creature, and I was conscious of being without one. He dispensed with my services and I was then able to call together all the members of the unit that could be found and work out some sort of plan in an attempt to create order out of chaos. Many of the wounded were still in the ambulances, some must have been there for a week or more, lying together with their dead comrades.

It was necessary to get the ambulances empty, the living put into tents in front of the château and the dead buried in the kitchen garden, their discs and identification cards handed to the sergeant in charge. Food and water were to be distributed at regular intervals and blankets and stretchers rearranged, changed and cleaned as supplies would allow. The remaining wounded in the château were to be moved out as the whole building was a shambles of fallen masonry, smashed windows, dirty dressings and all the other horrors of a broken down hygienic system.

On the second day after capture came a group of German medical officers and personnel. There was only one object to their ill-conceived visit, to collect details and photographs of the worst possible scenes of our hopeless and filthy state to be used for anti-British propaganda. As individuals they were rude, objectionable and inhuman and offered no help whatever in our meagre attempt at survival. They were like a pack of bloodhounds, hunting out the most vulnerable and horrifying aspects and responding by shouting at me or whoever happened to be nearest wearing British uniform. They were the only representatives of the Medical Services that visited us in France, which from the experience was no loss.

Suddenly at 19.00 hours fifty French ambulances arrived and everyone had to go. British stretchers in French ambulances presented great difficulty but everyone was anxious to get away from Rosendael so that two hundred and twenty wounded were packed in somehow before dark. Our destination was unknown but anywhere would seem preferable to what we were leaving. The unit crowded into the last three ambulances and the convoy was off. Fortunately I had been told that the journey was only four kilometres but the name of the place meant nothing. The men broke into song. It was the first time since leaving Proven two weeks before that they had been able to sit down with nothing to do.

The journey, though short in distance, was terrible. The ambulances were thrown from one side to the other as they jolted over partly filled shell holes. It was just another hell for the wounded. The sights of devastation along the road which ran behind the evacuation beaches where everything had been dumped were comparable to those at the base of the mole.

Eventually we arrived at Zuydcoote. It was a moonless night and unloading without a single light into strange surroundings was difficult. Our only contact with the authorities was a nurse who sat in a little room with one little candle. She had a saucepan of hot soup and a few phials of morphia, nothing else. It took us four hours to unload into various buildings and damaged tents, none of which had any resemblance to a ward although we were told that this was a military hospital. At 3.30 a.m. I dismissed the men and told them to get some sleep. At 4.00 a.m. we were all shouted at by the German guard and told to get up and parade. ''*Raus*, *'raus*, *'raus*!' It was the first time we had heard this call to action but it was soon to become a familiar background to prison life.

As the day developed the surroundings sorted themselves out. Zuydcoote was a large hospital on the dunes behind the beach. Apparently the place was full to bursting with seven thousand wounded and it soon became obvious that our unit, the last to arrive, and the only British element, was going to have to beg for its existence.

The outstanding priority became food. No one had eaten since midday the day before and we had no stores of our own. It was early afternoon before we managed to get some tubs of cooked beans. Having no utensils each patient took a handful and did what he could with the contents. The tubs were passed round until exhausted. Some of our patients were ill and a few very ill. There were two cases of tetanus and many of gas gangrene which gave primary concern. After hours of negotiation eighty of our worst cases were absorbed into the French wards, where nurses, beds and some drugs were available and it at once relieved the anxiety of being completely helpless. Gaze, our emeritus fellow, did pioneer work in the kitchens and achieved an unbelievable victory of being put on the kitchen staff. This subsequently had the invaluable effect of a regular supply of food to our patients.

Within a few days as the more lightly wounded were evacuated we got all our patients out of old torn tents and into wards. George Hewer and Willie Williamson as always spent every waking hour getting things for, attending to, or helping the patients in any possible way. One patient, Jimmy Langley, who had fought in the last rear-guard action with the Coldstream Guards, became an example for all. One morning I was called urgently to Lieutenant Langley, who had had a secondary haemorrhage from a compound fracture of the humerus. The patient seemed dead and was lying in a huge pool of blood. A piece of cotton held in front of his nose registered a slight flow of air.

Our orderlies had very little nursing experience but they knew the First Aid teaching of the benefits of a hot sweet cup of tea. One of them dashed off to get this remedy. When he returned the patient's head was raised a little and the cup brought to his lips. Hardly had they been moistened than the figure sat bolt upright and exclaimed, 'There's no bloody sugar in it!' The arm had to be amputated but on the third postoperative day Jimmy was out walking and putting his good arm through the railings begging for food. Within a month he had been transferred to Lille from where he escaped and eventually reached England, where he was enlisted onto the staff of MI9. He spent the war creating and maintaining the routes for escape and evasion in North-West Europe. Two in particular, the PAO (Pat) Line in the Eastern Pyrenees and the Comet Line in the West have become famous for assisting escaped prisoners of war and for the return home of pilots and air crew stranded in occupied territory.

Madame J de Launoy, a Belgian, determined to nurse the British, came with a small group of nurses and this at once raised our morale and changed the whole aspect of medical care. It was just what was required to jolt our psyches back into a glimmer of hope. They brought with them chocolates, sugar, shaving soap and other luxuries. Madame J de Launoy had nursed in the first war and knew Nurse Cavell very well. She had written a book entitled *Nurse in War Time*.

Another great friend during the survival period was the French Protestant curé. He held services in our wards and gave Communion to those who wished. He had a house in the compound and adopted our unit in a kindly paternal way and his influence was inestimable.

News of the war trickled through and it was all bad and at any time it was expected that the French would ask for a separate armistice. The French, who overwhelmed our existence, were universally depressed and convinced not only that they had lost the war but that Great Britain likewise would very soon be forced to sign an armistice; '*la même chose pour l'Angleterre*' they would say. Our French curé knew that we hoped for something better and allowed me to go to his house to listen to the British news. This was a unique privilege and he offered it at considerable risk to himself and his mother, who lived with him. Willie and I used to go down occasionally and knock at his side door just in time for the news bulletin. It would be answered by his old mother who would show us into the room where the wireless was kept.

As soon as the bulletin was over the set would be turned off and put away and the old lady would bring us in a cup of coffee. From there we would go to the wards and disseminate the news in a personal way.

By 15th June rumours of a French armistice were very strong and it seemed to us inevitable that Great Britain would follow. We had visions of returning home to a very changed Britain, in the not too distant future.

It was on 19th June when Willie and I returned once again for the bulletin that we heard to our astonishment and joy the speech of Winston Churchill reported from the House of Commons on the previous evening.

> If we can stand up to him, all Europe may be free and the life of the world may move forward into broad, sunlit uplands. But if we fail, then the whole world, including the United States, including all that we have known or cared for, will sink into the abyss of a new Dark Age, made more sinister, and perhaps more protracted, by the lights of perverted science. Let us therefore brace ourselves to our duties, and so bear ourselves that, if the British Empire and its Commonwealth last for a thousand years, men will still say: 'This was their finest hour'.

Quietly we returned to the wards, hiding our secretly won ebullience lest the source be leaked to unfriendly and jealous ears.

The information was slowly imparted to our own officer patients and from them to the rest of the unit. The boost in morale was another step up the ladder to our mental rehabilitation.

This was my first real taste of the greatness of the man. Was it possible that one person could turn the whole course of events from defeat into victory, but that is undoubtedly what he did during those few weeks after Dunkirk.

Little did I know that twenty-two years later it would be my privilege to operate on him for a fractured thigh bone.

The armistice with France was signed on 22nd June and from then on the Vichy Government was established in unoccupied France. After that, when our French friends said *'la même chose pour l'Angleterre'* I would shrug my shoulders and say *'je ne crois pas'*.

One of the last memories I have of Zuydcoote was a Sunday morning service taken by the curé. He had a special service in English printed with the hymns in full. Major Guy of the Green Howards read the first lesson and Willie the second. It was a service with intense meaning and purpose. The curé had exposed a real need and fostered it with tender care. Every square foot of the ward was crowded with people from other wards and the walls vibrated with vocal melody.

CHAPTER TWO
A Mother Superior

The vast groaning tension of accommodating and succouring seven thousand wounded with insufficient food, medical supplies and equipment under the recently acquired purgatory of captivity gradually subsided as increasing numbers were transferred away to camps and other hospitals. From the British unit the seriously ill had been admitted to the French wards where there were female nurses and possible access to the operating rooms and radiological department.

Early on the morning of 8th July a convoy of twenty patients left for an unknown destination and later that morning there was an order, which filtered through to me, that all remaining fracture cases requiring long periods in bed were to be loaded on to ambulances. At the last moment it became apparent that I was to go with them. In haste I gathered my things together, and searched out each of the Belgian nurses and the curé to say farewell and to thank them for their great service to our unit. George and Willie were nowhere to be found and just before the convoy moved off I got in with the driver of the leading ambulance.

Most of the patients that had been selected had fractures with open wounds of their thighs or legs; wounds which notoriously would take a long time to heal and needed prolonged bed-rest. The wounds were about five weeks old and it was not a good time to move them by ambulance, especially with the conditions of the roads as they were. I was very apprehensive about our destination and impressed on the driver the necessity for driving slowly over the bumps. He was a German soldier and entirely uncooperative and my ability to speak his language extremely limited. Above all, as the only doctor on the convoy, I should know the distance involved. The convoy should be stopped say every fifty kilometres so as to inspect the wounded and to give the orderlies a chance to report any trouble. Each of the other eight ambulances had a German guard, a French driver and one of our own orderlies in the back with the patients.

There was no let-up but the roads improved as we got into

Belgium where there had been less fighting.

I had another go at pumping the driver about our destination and got nowhere, but then decided to ask him how far, knowing sufficient German to get that question across. The reply came back, one hundred and fifty kilometres. This was of great interest and value because such a distance from Zuydcoote could not take us into Germany. It seemed preferable for the wounded to stay in a potentially friendly country until they were healed but of course it could be a stop for the night with a further journey the next day.

By early evening it became apparent that we were entering Brussels. Passing through the city I could recognise the buildings of the great International Exhibition of 1934. Sometime later the convoy halted outside the gates of a hospital and the German driver went off presumably to report our arrival. Outside the gate was a German sentry with a fixed bayonet. Parading up and down in the forecourt he looked the part with a grim unchangeable expression on his pale, emaciated face. Then for some reason he broke away from his beat and came toward our ambulance. For some moments he stood by my door giving me the impression that he had come to guard me personally while the driver was away. Then, turning his head slightly towards me he said:

'War's all over for you – ain't it?'

It was spoken in full cockney English. I couldn't believe what I had heard until he continued by saying:

'Yer'll be awright 'ere.'

The tendency to burst into laughter was acute but the delicacy of the relationship bade caution and asking him where he came from I was informed Ilford. He told me that he had come to Germany ten years previously for an engineering job in Hamburg and had spent a year in the army. We had come to the Hôpital Bruchmann and he thought it was likely that we would stay there and added that it was a good hospital. This was cheerful news. Our conversation lapsed and off went my fellow countryman to return to his strutting duties. Maybe he was thankful to be on the winning side, maybe he would rather have been back in Ilford, there was no indication, his expression was unchanged.

Half an hour later the gates opened and our convoy pulled up at one pavilion among many set in pleasant and well kept grounds.

I was released from my cabin and got out to meet a nursing sister at the door and from then on the whole scene changed. She was a Belgian and explained to me that the hospital was full of German wounded but for some reason it had been decided to fill one pavilion with British wounded and added that the Belgian staff would look after them. She showed me the wards. It was difficult to believe our luck. Here was a real hospital, just what our chaps needed and deserved. The journey had been worth while. Very soon our orderlies had put them all into bed and before long they were eating food the like of which they had not tasted since leaving home.

So precipitate was my inclusion in this convoy that I had had no opportunity to see the wounded individually or to know who of our unit was included. There were now only six out of thirty-five who had remained behind in Dunkirk: Sergeants Skelton and Beaumont and Privates Dyde, Evans, Trow and Woods.

The pavilion had other British wounded in adjoining wards but as far as could be seen there were none from Zuydcoote.

During the evening I had supper with a very pleasant Indian doctor called Aserapa and he told me about the medical set-up and organisation. He confirmed what the sister had said, that this was a hospital for German wounded but he explained that this pavilion, for British, was a show-place for visitors from neutral countries and representatives of the International Red Cross to demonstrate how well wounded prisoners were housed and treated. He told me that the surgeon-in-charge was a Belgian called Dumont who had had considerable experience of war surgery in the Spanish Civil War. The second-in-command was a lady physician called Mademoiselle Simon.

Later there was time to think about and dwell on the fantastic turn of events from the terrifying and appalling conditions the wounded had been through for nearly two months. It was hardly possible to believe our luck. Suddenly the responsibility of feeding and keeping alive hundreds of men fell away like a cloak of lead and there was nothing to do but to wait and watch. The high standard of nursing, the good food and excellent accommodation very soon had the most desirable effect on the morale of the patients.

Dumont who, under the Germans, was in charge of the pavilion, generally turned up during the latter half of the afternoon and everything revolved around his particular whims and fancies of the moment. He spoke seven languages fluently. His round would start about four o'clock and by six he had decided who was to be operated on. Work in the theatre often continued until midnight or later. He was a talented surgeon and had obviously had extensive experience in coping with anything during the years of the Spanish War. Not surprisingly he was inclined, as one would expect, to do things without or with insufficient anaesthetic. High standard anaesthetics were a British luxury not to be found on the Continent in the years between the wars. He was a dynamic character, restless and motivated to action. If he suddenly decided to operate he would walk down the hospital corridor and commandeer the first nurse or orderly to come and pour some chloroform on a mask. If there was no operating to do he would challenge any likely candidate to wrestle on the lawn.

Mademoiselle Simon was the perfect complement, always there, always helpful, kind and patient and abounding in common sense and feminine disposition.

She arrived at the hospital on a push-bike, wearing a large velours hat and from the moment she entered the building there was no lapse in the conversation. The welfare of the patients was her constant concern. She spent her time going from bed to bed attending not only to their medical condition but to their psychological and gastronomic needs as well.

I continued to look after the patients from our convoy. Fortunately they needed very little surgery but the conditions did wonders for them. Emaciated, pale, haggard men with wounds discharging pus and showing little sign of healing were converted within a few days into convalescent human beings with pink faces and a truculent repartee. The effect on the healing of their wounds was quite astounding.

Once a week there was a parade of honour for the wounded German heroes, consisting of a procession through the grounds of the hospital. A brass band, led by a band major and followed by a hundred or so German *Mädchen*, schoolgirls with arms full of flowers for the soldiers, passed from one pavilion to another and purposely gave ours the go by. Seeing me standing at the door in British uniform evoked a unified hissing noise from the young ladies but gave me an excellent opportunity of showing them the difference between a British salute and a Nazi airing of the armpit.

To Mademoiselle Simon I owe my life. One day, some two weeks or more after arriving at this haven, I felt ill and exhausted and took to my bed with a raised temperature, sore throat and swollen neck. Mademoiselle Simon came to see me and later that day brought along Dr Dumont. Both looked down my throat and I well remember Dumont telling Mademoiselle Simon that there was an abscess that was to be opened. I can remember wondering whether he would do it with or without an anaesthetic but before going to the theatre unconsciousness must have overtaken me and I remember no more. Later the story unfolded that Mademoiselle Simon had taken Dumont apart and told him that my throat was not to be cut. '*Non, non, non,*' she had said and he had walked away in disdain.

Mademoiselle Simon looked after me during my convalescence but never discussed the cause of my trouble. Some two or three weeks later, just before our unit was moved away from this hospital, I noticed an increasing weakness in my legs and inability to raise my feet to a right angle, a condition known as dropped feet, a typical late complication of diphtheria, and it suddenly dawned on me what the illness had been. Lancing the throat in the acute stages is invariably fatal and my gratitude to Mademoiselle Simon is eternal.

A screened-off corner was allocated to me and lying in the sun I was able to watch the swarms of planes forgathering during the early days of the Battle of Britain. It was pleasing to note how few of them seemed to return later in the day. The battle to destroy our defensive air force had officially started on '*Adlertag*' (Eagle Day), the 13th of August.

It was not surprising that this existence came to an end. While I was still practising walking with partially paralysed legs I got to hear in a roundabout way through the kitchen staff that we were leaving. No one in the pavilion had been informed but the delivery of rations that day had been cut and the conclusion was obvious. Next morning, sure enough, a convoy of trucks arrived and our status as exhibition pieces came abruptly to an end. Fortunately nearly all our men were mobile in plaster or with crutches and walking was possible. The few still in bed were left behind. The staff of the Hôpital Bruchmann and the rations had put us on our way to cope with what was to come.

We were bundled into the lorries and away we went, destination unknown.

An hour or so later, driving into a large town, the convoy pulled up outside some formidable iron gates slung inside a forbidding stone arch. The gates were opened by a guard and we drove into a barracks alive with German soldiers. Eventually after hanging about for two hours, awaiting orders, we were off-loaded into what were obvious stables. Many other wounded were already there from other parts of France. Their state and conditions of accommodation were appalling. They looked so terrible beside our men and were lying in wooden boxes with straw on wire netting for mattresses. Our patients and men were horrified at what they saw. It made them feel almost indecent to look so well among their half-starved comrades. The shape of things to come pervaded us all with horror.

A few recognitions across the barrier soon broke the ice and before long we had come to realise that we were all in it together and were soon learning fast the truth about life in a German barracks. The town was Mechelen (Malines) halfway between Brussels and Antwerp, and in counting our blessings we were fortunate still to be surrounded by a friendly population who we learnt were constantly trying to smuggle in some extra food.

It became apparent after a few days, that there were some British wounded in the Civilian Hospital and someone had suggested to the Germans that British doctors should be allowed to visit them. For some unknown reason the request rang a bell and two of us were ordered to go to the hospital. This proved to be a great asset for us and a help to the patients to see doctors who spoke their own language, but, like the others, they needed above all sympathetic nursing and adequate food rather than any special medical or surgical treatment.

Ralph Gunderson and I were escorted by a German guard three times a week. It was a walk of about a mile and on arrival at the hospital the guard would see us past the main door and then disappear, presumably to the guard quarters.

The hospital was nursed by nuns and it was into their tender care that we were transferred and their responsibility to pass us back to the guard when our work was done. It was certainly an excellent arrangement as we were soon to learn.

On the first morning we were taken by one of the nuns to meet the Mother Superior in her office. She greeted us very cordially and told us about the patients in the wards. There were quite a number, about twenty of whom were British. There was a Belgian doctor in charge of all the wards but the Mother Superior added emphatically that he would be delighted for us to advise or do anything we wished in the way of changing dressings or plasters.

The wards had that continental, medieval touch with a blue tinge from the windows and a rather dim and chastening atmosphere, bereft of any cheer or sparkle. There were no flowers or decorations and the few pictures were religious. But the sparkle came from the nuns and was reflected from their patients who thrived with their care and attention. It was a great joy to meet and chat with the patients and to listen to their stories because most of them had not seen a British doctor since the time of wounding during the early days of the invasion of Belgium. The majority were convalescent but still needed encouragement, nursing and nourishment, which they were obviously getting in abundance.

The ladies of the town maintained a continual pressure to get extra food to them and it came in all sorts of ways. The voluminous habit of a nun could hide a great deal and visitors to the local Belgian sick and wounded were adept at acting as carriers. The German guard, on the other hand, became increasingly determined to stop the communication between civilians and prisoners of war.

One morning on arrival, when our escort was passing us through the entrance, a Belgian woman, with a quick step and a large parcel under her arm, approached the main gate. The sentry lowered his rifle, pointing the bayonet towards her.

'*Eingang verboten!*' he shouted.

Our good friend clutched the bayonet with her gloved hand, lifted the gun, gave him a kiss on the cheek and walked in.

It was customary to spend an hour or so in the wards and then another period in the dressing and plaster room, making things more comfortable. X-rays were available to check the position of fractures or foreign bodies but on the whole there was little to do and by midday our work was generally finished. The Mother Superior decided that any spare time, waiting for the guard to take us back, could be well spent in the library delving into the medical literature available.

It was a room entirely walled with well seasoned bookshelves except for the one door. The shelves were all full and the books showed little evidence of recent disturbance. There was a large central oak table at which we were invited to sit and presumably read but there was no literature available on the table. The nun, who had brought us there, produced some medical periodicals from a drawer and put them out with a smile and then hurried off with purposeful steps. We sat there in studious silence, reading a bit and musing a bit, wondering about our next move and when the guard would fetch us.

Within a few minutes the door opened and in came two nuns each with a tray of eating utensils and a glass of red wine. One of them explained that we could have lunch provided there were no

Germans in the centre of the hospital. In the event of the guard coming for us or of an inspection it would be known very quickly, the trays would be taken away and we should be found reading at the table. It was explained how necessary it was to keep everything on the tray in case swift action became necessary. The periodicals were put in a neat pile close to our trays. It needed no encouragement to cotton on to this idea and as the plan unfolded it became obvious that the details had been contrived by a master mind – we presumed the Mother Superior.

There is no need to describe the lunch. It was wholesome, well-cooked and served with affection. What greater joy could they have given us?

This, to our delight, became a routine for each visit. One day the alarm did go. The nuns entered quickly and with the minimum commotion within seconds had pushed both trays into a large cupboard and there we were dutifully reading medical magazines. The German passed our door to visit the Mother Superior but we saw nothing more of him and when he had gone we were allowed to continue. It made us appreciate the efficiency of the look-out system on guard while we were allowed to lunch in peace.

One day we were told by one of the priests visiting the wards that messages could be collected from all patients and personnel. It was hoped that they would reach the United Kingdom and on arrival be distributed by post. No mention was made as to how it was to be done or who was to collect them but it was up to us to bring them to the hospital packed as tightly as possible by Thursday of next week. Each message was to be written on a piece of paper 10 cm by 10 cm and folded into four. It should show clearly the name and place for delivery and a message of no more than twenty words. It was obviously the responsibility of Gunderson and me to make this valuable opportunity known personally to every prisoner in the barracks and then to collect and deliver them at the right time.

When the day came the messages were neatly bound into four small packages and we walked to hospital with one strapped to each armpit. They remained there during the ward round with Sister and when we had finished she took us to her room and produced another small packet of messages from the twenty chaps in the different wards. She had no idea of how they were to be collected. Like us she had had no mention of their disposal. It would be a pity if they misfired because it was probable that no one in Britain knew if we were alive or dead. Doubtless all of us were posted as missing and these messages would at least let our families know that we were still in this world.

Then all of a sudden we knew. While walking in the corridor to the library we were confronted by a priest with a very red face and a large hat. He came close and said, 'You av ze papers?' Fortunately by then we had transferred them to our jacket pockets and handing over was easy. They disappeared into a large pocket inside his ample cloak, something rather similar to a poacher's pouch. Within a few seconds, anxious it would seem to avoid any unnecessary conversation or even to be seen talking to us, he had sidled past and was off down the corridor.

Some days later the news filtered through from the nuns that someone had contemplated sailing a boat across the North Sea at night but there was never any confirmatory evidence then or later that any of the messages had got home. However the thought that an effort to get news through was being made raised the morale of the prisoners and came as a fascinating revelation to witness the lengths our ecclesiastical mentors were prepared to take risks to help us in adversity.

One day Ralph and I had a difficult decision to make. The Mother Superior let it be known to us, through one of her senior sisters, that we could be hidden in the convent so that it would seem that we had escaped from the hospital and got out into the town. Apparently there was a huge store of potatoes in the cellar and it was explained that we could be hidden in a large box, which would be covered over with potatoes, while the search was active.

The audacity amazed us. It was another plan of a master mind and the message conveyed was obviously entirely sincere and conducive to action. We stood in silence looking at the sister and then decided to discuss it over lunch.

It was of course a most attractive offer requiring considerably more courage on the part of the Mother Superior than by us. However a decision had to be made and on contemplation it became clear that it was impossible to accept.

Ralph and I were virtually on medical parole as soon as we were out of the camp. There had been no exchange of signed cards but to escape under the circumstances would be very bad propaganda. It would undoubtedly stop any further medical visits to the hospital and would almost certainly be used in future as an argument against medical parole of any sort. We still had a duty to our patients. Ralph spoke German quite well and he had impressed on them the importance of the patients in the Civilian Hospital being visited by their own doctors.

There was another factor which became very prominent, which the Mother Superior had not taken into account. Had we been found during the search she would almost certainly have been shot or sent to a political camp in Germany, for elimination.

We knocked on her door and were welcomed in.

Our answer was expressed in a non-specific way, thanking her for her great kindness and consideration. We explained about medical parole and our moral obligation to return to the Camp. She could have smiled sweetly, nodded and left it at that, but not a bit of it. The plan was described in some detail and then she took us down beneath the Convent for an inspection of the cellar. There was a large pile of potatoes and another stack of boxes and cases. It would be possible to be covered from view but once suspicion had arisen to the extent of searching the cellars there would be not much chance of avoiding discovery.

Her invitation was undoubtedly sincere. I had met the same daring detachment and resolve in the nuns in Dunkirk. It needed a stiff upper lip to deny her motivation and to take, as it were, the easy way out. The little party walked back to her room in silence. I looked at Ralph and saw him shake his head and there was little doubt in my mind that it was not on.

The Mother Superior sat in her chair and looked at us. It was a difficult moment. I expressed again our great gratitude and explained about the repercussions if parole was broken. She was obviously very disappointed at our decision and the meeting broke up leaving us with a feeling of chicken-livered impotence.

Malines, at that time, was full of activity. The German army was preparing for the invasion of Britain as the natural conclusion of conquering Western Europe.

In the barracks, where we were housed, our men had seen German troops jumping into the deep end of the swimming bath, laden with full equipment and having to swim and get out. Flat-bottomed barges were being constructed in great quantity and the ports were full of them. Maps appeared on the walls of the barracks of the great offensive through Western Europe with indications that Britain was the next step. In scale the North Sea was shown as a narrow channel, no more than three or four kilometres wide. The average German was quite ignorant of the North Sea and Channel and not motivated in any way, at that time, to the war of bridgeheads and amphibious techniques. He was a land-conquering machine and probably very frightened of water. These

Officers in Sotteville Camp awaiting repatriation

Jock Finlayson in Oflag V11/C

maps suggested, with a single arrow, the ease of crossing the North Sea.

Someone in Britain at that time had a brilliant idea. The counter-invasion offensive of bombing the French and Belgian ports had not started, but thousands and thousands of miniature bathing costumes were dropped over the coastal areas. This was a stroke of genius, of far greater psychological impact than the quantity of pamphlets that had filtered down through the clouds. To the Belgians it appealed tremendously and became a much needed nucleus for laughter in an otherwise grim world.

One of our men died in the barracks and the senior officer was informed that he would be buried in a local cemetery. A request for a number of men to attend the funeral service was surprisingly granted. For those wishing to go the order was to parade inside the main entrance at an allocated time.

There must have been about fifty of us. We were marched to the church under heavy guard and seated in the centre block of seats in the nave. The other blocks of seats were filled with Belgian civilians and the German guards. It was a simple service which passed off without any incidents. After it was over all remained seated awaiting the next move. There was some commotion going on at the back of the church and before the guard had time to call us to order two curtains parted and out came trays of pewter tankards jubilantly transported by our Belgian friends. They were full of beer and passed round first to the guards and then to the prisoners with such nonchalance that one would assume such a procedure to be the accepted conclusion to a military funeral service in this ancient Belgian Archbishopric. It was a great triumph for our Belgian friends, ever watchful for a chink in the armature of the guard that isolated us from generous aid. Possibly it is unrivalled in the annals of church rituals.

As we assembled in the aisle, leaving the empty tankards in the pews, there were hosts of friendly smiles and giggles. How wise it was to have included the guard, otherwise our return journey would undoubtedly have been a shouting match. It was a welcome climax to a sad occasion and a fitting send off for our imminent departure.

Within a few days the rumour of a move came through and although it seemed obvious that it would be into Germany the news was nevertheless a relief. The conditions in the stables, in close proximity to an active training base preparing to invade our country was demoralising. Rations were hopelessly inadequate and the beds really little more than straw on stone cobbles.

That morning, soon after dawn, saw a bedraggled, unkempt and emaciated party of men being herded into position by shouting goons. Officers were separated into one group and the rest into five sections. Each had to be counted and checked and counter-checked. It was nearly an hour before the procession moved off amidst more shouting.

At the station there were more goons waving their arms and shouting. Our party was jammed into two empty coaches, but we were thankful to be in a proper passenger train and not cattle trucks.

It was getting dark and the train jogged along and halted. It started up again and jogged on a bit more and then stopped. For the next hour nothing happened, we sat there on a siding but there was no platform.

Then suddenly the goons decided that we had to get off in all speed. *'Raus, 'raus, 'raus* reverberated down the line. Gradually we shouldered and handled our parcels and packages and climbed down the side of the carriage to reach the ground. The noise from the goons continued, turned on at the slightest provocation, like a gaggle of geese. Slowly they manoeuvred us into some semblance of a marching order, but they were the ones who had to do the hard work, not us. Our turn was to come. Slowly the party got under way and the question foremost in many of our minds after walking for an hour was how much further. The guards certainly would not give us any indication, almost certainly from arrogance not ignorance.

Not knowing the distance created an element of apprehension. We had all heard of the forced marches into Germany, and were scared lest this might be the start of something similar. Nearly everyone, except for the two lucky doctors, were badly under-nourished and some of them still had unhealed wounds. Many of them were trying to carry too much and the outlook for the night was not good.

Over on our right there were some ack-ack shells exploding and planes were audible. It was not clear what was happening until we heard crunch, crunch in the distance. It was my idea of where Frankfurt should be and it was undoubtedly an air raid. It could have come from nowhere else than Britain.

Air raids, in those days, meant more to the British than to the Boche, the old familiar sounds and the disastrous effects beneath were second nature to us. To hear this now in Germany was nectar to our morale and at the best possible moment. Suddenly it put a purpose to it all, our packages became lighter and our steps less laboured.

Within two hours we halted in the grounds of a large house. It was approached by a narrow, winding country road and seemed, as far as could be seen in the dark, isolated from other buildings. Inside every square yard of space in the rooms and corridors was crammed with iron bedsteads. The only room with space was that allocated for eating. A mattress and one blanket could be drawn from a store and this meant a great deal of jostling in confined spaces. By midnight mattresses had been distributed by the orderlies and everyone had at least something to lie on and compared to the cobbles and straw of the stables there was little difficulty in getting to sleep.

The next morning early we were roused by shouts from the guard. Every man had to put all his kit on his bed and stand by it. Men of the Gestapo circulated and searched everything. They took anything of value such as watches, fountain pens, and in fact anything that seemed to interest them. Our Senior Officer objected very strongly but he was told that these articles were only being confiscated temporarily; but of course we knew differently as no records of ownership had been taken down. For two hours we stood by our beds until the Gestapo had found all they wanted and after that we were free to circulate. Everywhere was crammed full but it was an excellent opportunity to meet old friends and pool all our knowledge of what had happened since the balloon went up. Gradually it became possible to arrange some order so that the convalescent wounded were housed separately from the RAMC personnel and the officers separately from the men. The whole place had been barbed wired off, leaving insufficient space in the grounds for any reasonable exercise. Meagre rations were issued in the dining room and it soon became apparent that life here was neither dangerous nor treacherous but boring, frustrating, with nothing constructive to do and very little to eat. Apart from walking round in a circle in the diminutive patch of garden there were only three possibilities, to sit on your bed, lie on your bed or sit on someone else's bed. Fortunately there were some packs of cards and these became the raison d'être of life at Dieburg.

Command of the place had been given to a local doctor, a diminutive type with a small-man complex. He had the rank of *Oberstabsarzt* and wore a long grey cloak with a red silk lining. He liked to assemble the doctors and padres in the dining room and give them a pep talk. Nothing could have been more nauseating than the disciplinary outbursts by this pompous little man. On one occasion he stated that he would allow no meetings, religious or otherwise, of more than ten persons at any time.

This came as a culmination of a series of talks of Nazi propaganda and infantile ideas about prisoner of war discipline and it had a most astounding effect. Quite spontaneously all the padres, whether Anglican, Roman Catholic, Presbyterian or whatever, got together and planned a combined service. It was held in the largest ward on the following day. There was a constructed altar one end and the padres sat on a row of beds either side. The room was filled to bursting and the singing, needless to say, was full throttle. One padre of each denomination was standing by the altar and they took turns in conducting the service. It was a vivid demonstration of the reaction to religious suppression. The guards failed to interfere but all hell was let loose verbally by the little doctor in his red-lined cloak that afternoon but no punitive action was taken; maybe he was apprehensive of the consequences.

One wet, cold Sunday afternoon comes back as a vivid memory. There were six of us attached to a very worn pack of cards, playing bridge and taking it in turns to sit out and watch, seated as we were all around one bed. In the camp was a great personality, W.E. Tucker (Bill), one time Captain of English rugger, and for no apparent reason Bill produced a tin of sardines out of his pocket. It was a sight impossible to believe. Slowly and deliberately he opened the tin and there in succulent oil were six sardines. With a teaspoon we ate one each, very slowly and tastefully. How Bill had got it through many searches by the Gestapo and why he should produce it at that particular moment, refraining from saving it for when he was alone and eating all of his due, was beyond our conception. It was the whitest act of all time, but typical of his generous, open hearted nature.

Dieburg was nothing more than a transit camp and mercifully it was not destined that we should stay there for always, the boredom and lack of space would have finished us off once the faces on the packs of cards had worn out. How or why we were allocated to different camps was as always an unknown factor but a small group of doctors and padres were separated off one November morning and away we went. George, Willie and I, the three of us from Dunkirk, were all together again which was a great joy. There were about twenty of us in the party with four guards.

It was a long day in the train which mostly ambled along at something under thirty miles an hour and stopped for long periods. By far the greatest interest, out of the window, was evidence of bombing. Almost subconsciously our eyes searched for this or any circumstantial evidence to support our cupidity. We would have no hesitation in sitting in the train for hours and hours or even days provided we thought this to be the cause of delay.

In the evening we were hustled out of the train to stand on the platform until the next lot of orders came through. It was a moderate walk to the camp. In the middle of a village we halted outside some extensive barbed wire gates with two guards to check us in. It was dark and we were unable to see very much but one got the impression of a courtyard half surrounded by buildings and the rest of the perimeter a formidable double barbed wire fence which was flood-lit, at that particular time, presumably to cover the disturbance of our arrival.

Inside the camp we were met by a member of the staff and taken to the dining room, the *Speisesaal*. A British officer turned up to advise us where beds were vacant.

We were split up into small gangs and eventually three of us were taken to a room with five double-tier bunks. George Hewer and I were together. It was after midnight and sleep was more important than anything else, with the exception of food and there was no hope of any form of nourishment at that hour. The meagre ration of black bread, meat paste and one cup of ersatz coffee had been finished on the train.

The bed was a wooden box-like affair with movable bed boards, a thin palliasse and one blanket. I climbed into the top bunk with George below and knew no more.

By 6.45 a.m. the room was alive with people getting out of bed. Finding three strangers in what had been empty bunks our roommates explained that *Appell* was at seven, for which one had to be dressed and down in the courtyard. It was not necessary to shave, just to put on some clothes and come down. It could take as long as an hour so it was as well to wrap up as much as possible.

The twenty newcomers were fitted into the ranks and we stood there watching the counting going on. There must have been over two hundred officers in all with about twenty orderlies and it was fascinating and infuriating to see what a business they made of it. It was an introduction to static, officer, prisoner of war life. Mountains were made out of molehills because there were no mountains.

This morning there was the additional complication of fitting in and counting twenty new officers. It took about half an hour, a job which could easily have been done in five minutes by a couple of alert guards, but the advantage of a speedy solution was obviously dubious. It would release twenty-five minutes of boredom with very little hope of anything of note happening. A parade where one could shout and search for anything wrong with the hope of shouting more was a far better pastime and there was sadistic pleasure in creating unnecessary discomfort.

The guards saluted their officers, indicating that they had impressed them that the count was correct and the parade broke up. It was now breakfast time and we were led to the dining room by one of our room-mates. Everyone of the established inhabitants it seemed carried a cardboard box under his arm. It was the container of a British Red Cross parcel used for keeping any food, eating utensils, mug, flavouring agents, etc., and carried between the bunkroom and dining room. It was the hall mark of a prisoner of war going to or coming from a meal. It was natural cardboard in colour with a white label showing the insignia of the Red Cross and the Order of Saint John.

This camp was one of two at Spangenberg in Hesse, about twenty miles south of Kassel. The upper camp was in a *Schloss* on top of a hill and the inmates were predominantly Naval officers. The lower camp, known as Elbersdorf, was in the village beside a small river and its inmates were almost entirely Army officers. Both camps collectively were known as IX A/H.

On 17th February 1941, five doctors were posted to other camps, destination and purpose unknown. George Hewer, Bill Davidson and I finished up in an empty cigar factory, which we were told was being prepared as a convalescent unit to receive British wounded. We could hardly believe our luck with good accommodation and rations sufficient to sustain us without Red Cross parcels which were unlikely to arrive at a new address under three months.

The guarding and the barbed wire surround were perfunctory compared to Elbersdorf but again we were committed to the care of wounded and therefore virtually on medical parole. Escape from the unit would be possible but it was deep in the centre of Germany and our conscience was not free to go.

Two days later the party arrived, consisting of convalescent wounded from the 51st Highland Division which had been surrounded at St Valéry-en-Caux. With the patients were three doctors and some medical personnel. The wounded were on the whole mostly recovered and healed but needed building up before going to work on the land or in the factories. With our own orderlies and reasonable rations this presented no obvious difficulty.

The three doctors accompanying the wounded had found out that they were not going to stay there but were being sent to Spangenberg. Captain Dicky came to my room carrying in his hand a little attache case; he opened it and to my horror and excitement I realised it was a wireless set.

'What am I going to do with this?' he said. I was so amazed that he could walk in carrying a radio in his hand and thinking hard said:

'You will never get it into Spangenberg. On arrival you will be taken to the guard quarters where you will be told to take everything off and to put your baggage and clothes together. While you have a shower everything will be searched. You will then be inspected for rashes etc., and when cleared told to dress again. There is no possibility of getting away with it.'

'What shall I do, it seems a pity to lose it?'

'Leave it here,' I said. 'We can probably conceal it in this accommodation.'

He sat still and thought and said nothing.

A half an hour later it was time for them to go.

Dicky looked at me and said, 'I think I shall take it.'

'You're crazy,' said I without the slightest hesitation and my reaction was entirely genuine although I had already counted on it as a fascinating and valuable challenge.

I watched him walk off to the van with the guard and two other officers carrying the little case together with a large one in one hand and steadying a large pack on his back with the other.

Thank God he stuck to his decision. I found the whole story out much later. On arrival at the camp they were taken to the place for examination and just inside the door, Dicky going in last of the three, following the guard, noticed a radiator. He pushed the little case on the floor behind it and then went on to strip and doubtless every bit of his luggage was gone through. Finally as he left, again last behind the guard, with his free hand he snatched it back and walked into the main camp carrying his radio.

That radio became the mouthpiece throughout Germany. It was taken over by two or three experts and a special hiding place made for it. Every evening it was brought out under the protection of spyhole-intelligence, and the news taken down in shorthand. Readers then went round every room to give a daily news service. Not only did the inmates of Elbersdorf have a daily bulletin but as doctors and padres, in particular, moved around the various camps, a *précis* of the news for three months or so was taken.

Unfortunately it became apparent some time later that there were prisoners in the camp who knew more about the events of the war than the German army or the German papers. Some fool had let slip news that was slow coming through and the assumption became obvious, that there was a receiving set in the camp. Extensive searches were made but it was extremely cleverly hidden and was never out of its hole when there was a German inside the compound. The set was not found.

Some time later the camp heard that it was to be moved to Poland as a reprisal for the bad treatment of German officers in Canada. Determination to find the radio may have been a deciding factor.

The order was that all baggage not essential for the journey and any other equipment was to be placed in the guard store room three days before departure. The problem of what to do with the radio was a difficult one.

In the camp was a large medicine ball. This was quite a heavy affair used for throwing to each other in the compound for exercise. It was a very familiar sight and well known to the guard. The medicine ball with all other sporting equipment was handed into the guard.

It was hoped that they did not know that there were two identical balls. The second one was unpicked, the radio dismantled and its parts distributed throughout the ample padding and the ball repaired.

In the middle of the night the lock of the guard store was picked and the medicine balls changed. The first was hidden back in the camp under the floorboards and the second went off to Poland without any difficulty. The set once again received very careful attention from the experts, was reassembled so that once more it was able to provide its fantastic daily service. Its new home was Strafe Lager, Fort XV, Thorn, Poland.

CHAPTER THREE
Try, Try Again

As the number of patients diminished it became obvious to our hosts that three British doctors were an unnecessary embarrassment and it was my lot to be transferred elsewhere. Bill Davidson was left in charge. He had developed a very absorbing pastime for which there was limitless opportunity. It was colloquially known as flogging the bishop. He was meticulously carving a set of chessmen out of any bits of hard wood he could lay his hands on. Evening after evening, as we read or slept, Bill, with a few oddments of carving tools, would flog away creating an incredibly handsome set of chessmen.

I left early in the morning with a single German guard and spent the day mucking about in trains and stations and arrived in the evening, at a hospital in Schleiz, a little town near Plauen on the Czechoslovakian border. The hospital was a jumble of buildings in the centre of the town surrounded by a double barbed wire fence with a sentry patrol. At the main door there was a guard unit, past which we were let in. Inside it was a joy to meet three other RAMC doctors, Crook, Dearlove and Fox.

This was a two hundred-bedded hospital for prisoners of war, working, over a large district, on the land, in factories, and many on constructing aerodromes. It served a vast work force comprised, almost entirely, of British, French and Yugoslavs. It was our job to see anyone who was brought to the out-patient department and to decide whether admission was advisable or to attempt to give some help with a very meagre assortment of medical supplies.

The German medical officer for the district had an office and surgery in the hospital. He saw none of the prisoner of war patients himself but his signature was essential for admission to hospital. This was the rub. So many of the men that came up for examination were tired out and needed a rest and admission for a week or so would have been a very valuable relief, but the vital signature was not so easily obtained. An indefinite diagnosis such as exhaustion, chronic fatigue or psychiatric upset, was unacceptable. A diagnosis of pneumonia, acute bronchitis, quinsy, influenza or more unusual complaints had to be backed by clinical findings and these were liable to be checked. A raised temperature was generally sufficient but could easily be repeated and he was liable to ask his own orderly to do so. There was one test above all that appealed to him as a true indication of illness, the blood sedimentation rate. If a column of blood is set upright in a tube the corpuscles gradually settle down and produce a lower column of sediment and a column of clearer serum above. If the blood is allowed to settle for one or two hours a normal person will show a small degree of sedimentation whereas a patient with a general or local infection or other serious illness will show an accelerated rate. Almost invariably our German boss would ask for the result of the sedimentation rate and sometimes want to be shown it standing in the tube. Fortunately he had never been known to ask his own orderly to repeat it. It was possible that he did not know how or that he was unprepared to wait for an hour for the result.

This was a valuable source of subterfuge because an increased rate rang a bell in his administrative mind and the signature was invariably forthcoming. It was a valuable asset because an increased sedimentation could quite easily be obtained artificially and so let a person into hospital who needed rest. With this trump card up our sleeve there was some latitude but we had to be careful not to play it too often. One of our orderlies in the out-patients' surgery was very skilled at this trick and could produce an increased rate whenever the evidence was needed.

At that time of year in May and June the pressure on the hospital had slackened and once a patient had been admitted there seemed to be no urgency for discharge.

Dearlove had been there longer than the other two British doctors and he argued that if anyone was going to escape it was his turn. He was South African and spoke Afrikaans naturally and German with considerable ease. He openly resented having joined the Royal Army Medical Corps to spend years in prisoner of war camps and hospitals and allowed his Boerish anti-British venom to flow freely towards us, but he had a very large tongue curled up in a cheek of humour which some years later was reflected in his contributions to *Punch* from his home in Dorset. Dizzy Dearlove was determined to have a go at escape and we all endorsed this plan because the medical work could easily be covered by one or two doctors. There was no question of off duty. We were there on call always and the beds were by no means full.

The plan was to let him down on two sheets tied together so that he could swing round the corner of the wall on to the slate roof of a building two stories lower. Once on this roof he should be able to walk on his heels with his back flat to the wall for about ten yards which would bring him to another wall at right angles and edging the road. There were two sentries patrolling the hospital and it would be a matter of jumping down in between their beats.

The day planned was Sunday, 22nd June, and we had everything prepared for that night. The length of the night was minimal as it was the longest day of the year but it was warm for sleeping out, food was growing in the fields and Dearlove, with his adequate German and suitable clothes, planned to walk during daylight.

Little did we know that he had chosen a day to become momentous in world history. At dawn Germany invaded Russia and thus tore up the Soviet–German non-aggression pact which had been signed in Moscow on the previous 23rd August by Von Ribbentrop and Molotov in the presence of Stalin. So stunned was Stalin with this unbelievable treachery that it took him several days to order the Red Army to resist.

At eleven that night Dearlove disappeared through the window backwards, with his rucksack on his tummy and the strap round his neck. We let him down with the sheets until he could touch the lower roof and hook himself round the corner with his right foot. In stony silence we listened and heard some scraping and then some pieces clattering on the slate roof below. Nothing more happened, the tension on the sheet remained tight and it moved as he turned himself round. The roof on which he was standing sloped away gradually from the higher wall but there was a ledge adjoining the wall about nine inches wide and it was along this that he had to walk on his heels with his back to the wall, holding his rucksack in front of him.

Ten minutes later the sheet went slack and swung back to hang vertical from our window. There was no more sound from him – indicating that he was all right. The sheet was pulled up and we both knelt there at the window listening.

This way out from the building had been chosen because there was no barbed wire fence to negotiate. There were no windows on the road side so that it meant negotiating the slate sloping roof to get to the road wall. Once there it was merely a matter of hanging and dropping – a height of twelve feet, at a moment when both sentries were out of sight. We listened and listened. There was noise suggestive of plaster falling on to the slate and then silence. Five minutes later we heard him drop down on to the road. There was no challenge, no shouting as we continued with our ears cocked in readiness. Nothing happened to disturb the night. He must be away.

The administrative head of the hospital was the Quartermaster, an officer of comparatively junior rank but a prominent Nazi official and all-powerful within the hospital. He was in charge of all the stores which took up considerable space.

On Sundays it was his habit to take coffee with us at mid morning and he would arrive in a resplendent white uniform, obviously very pleased with his sartorial elegance. He had some academic respect for our profession and had a friendly approach. This Sunday as usual he was dressed in white but something was on his mind and over coffee he told us that Germany had invaded Russia. We sat in silence and thought; there was little to say. He left us for his stores and later I called on him because there was something needed for a fractured femur. To my amazement, and to his horror, he was trying on a British battle dress. It was a severe shock to us both and I retreated in great haste.

On Monday morning there was no sign of Dearlove. We had prepared our story for the occasion. The news would break probably during the course of the morning. The Quartermaster was very much on more friendly terms with him than the rest of us. He spoke German and had potentially an anti-British element in his discussion which our host had not failed to detect.

He would undoubtedly want Dearlove during the course of the day, and we waited for the balloon to burst. As there was no sign of his return it was an indication that he had got out of the neighbourhood. Tony Crook and Foxy, like me, had all made ourselves scarce in our wards during the morning hoping to avoid the explosion.

To our surprise we met at lunch and none of us had been tackled by the Quartermaster. No news was good news as far as Dearlove was concerned, but it was possible that he had been picked up and the Quartermaster knew all about it.

Then just at the end of our meal in came the Quartermaster.

'*Wo ist Dearlove*?' he said in a quiet voice.

There was no answer.

'*Wo ist er*?' in a somewhat more strained voice.

'We don't know,' said Tony, 'he was not here when we got up this morning.'

'Not here,' he said in a louder voice. 'When did you see him last?'

'Last night. We all went to bed and this morning he was not there.'

'He has escaped.' This time it was a shout with an intense concern on his face.

'You know where he is, don't you?'

'No', I said, 'I have no idea.'

The Quartermaster turned about and left the room. Doubtless he was off to see the guard and give them hell.

The cat was now out of the bag, which was a relief, and there was, as before, nothing to do except to wait and see. We had to be prepared for a visit from the Gestapo and a search of all our belongings. There was no need to be a prisoner of war for long to develop this instinct as an automatic reflex. What form it would take with three doctors and what reprisals would be known to us before long.

Sure enough that afternoon we were summoned to our room to meet the Quartermaster and a colleague, presumably from the local military police office and a police sergeant.

All of us stuck to the same story, that Dearlove went to bed that night and was not there in the morning. We had no idea whatever of his intention.

In a loud voice the visitor accused us of being liars, with some justification, but got no further than that as regards when or where he had got out. We had been told to put all our possessions out on our beds. These were inspected by the Sergeant in a very perfunctory way but Dearlove's bed, locker and drawers were searched with great care. There was infinite opportunity in the hospital for hiding anything to avoid inspection and this they obviously realised. It was probable that the local police had no experience in dealing with prisoners of war and escapers. However they left and no reprisals were taken. It was just possible that the fleeting incident in the store on the previous day had placed the Quartermaster in a vulnerable position and that he was anxious to make as little as possible of the whole business.

No news whatever about Dearlove got back to us. If he had been recaptured it is almost certain that the Quartermaster would have been delighted to tell us. Within a few days another doctor arrived to fill the gap. There were many doctors idle in the Officer Camps, they were expendable and most of them pleased to be transferred to a place where there was something to do clinically.

Tony Crook was a regular officer and carried the distinction of upholding the disciplinary part of his vocation as well as his professional ability and responsibility. He had it in mind, very clearly, that it was the duty of a captured soldier to escape or try to escape, whenever possible, so as to retain the maximum number as guards as possible. The more trouble prisoners created the greater the force needed to contain them. He invited me to join him and we discussed the idea at length. Were we professionally at liberty to escape and leave our patients? That was the main deterrent. On the other hand it was our duty to escape and to try and get back home where doctors were badly needed. There was an unlimited supply of idle doctors here very willing to take our place as had recently been shown.

We decided to go and worked out a route. Our knowledge of the local geography was negligible but we had a map of Central Europe torn out of a general atlas. It had been shown to me by one of the patients who had found it in his work camp. His unit was housed in a building that was previously a school and he had come across an atlas and torn out the essential page. I showed great interest and he said, 'You have it, I shall never need it.' 'I don't suppose I shall,' I replied, but nevertheless it was an attractive offer and I agreed to borrow it and study it carefully out of interest. It was a small scale of 30 kilometres to the centimetre. It showed the small towns, rivers and railways and frontiers.

We had both been out locally with the German doctor in his car to inspect the chaps at the local *Arbeits Kommandaturs* and we had deduced that the local railway ran somewhere east of us and our map showed a place called Hof about thirty kilometres away. This railway we could see ran down towards Salzburg through Regensburg. The Swiss border was about 500 kilometres away by the route we meant to adopt. The idea was to make for the Salzburg area and then approach Switzerland through the Tyrol. We had no German money so that it meant a long walk, unless we could jump a goods train or hide in a lorry. Food was not a great problem. It would be possible to save and borrow enough to keep us going for ten to fourteen days. We both had a reserve of sugar, chocolate, condensed milk and biscuits from Red Cross parcels. It was summer time, warm for sleeping out and there should be food available on the land.

Neither of us spoke German at all well so we decided to be foreign workers and selected Polish slaters as a choice. We had no papers of any sort and had to avoid controls like the plague. It would mean covering most of the distance in the hours of darkness and hiding up in the crops or woods during the day.

At the end of July or early August there were about nine hours of darkness and we optimistically reckoned to cover thirty-five to forty kilometres a day. That would bring us to the Salzburg area in nine to ten days and after that through the mountains to the Swiss border we hoped to be able to walk during the day. It would need a lot of luck.

We shook hands on it but before making a definite decision agreed to take our colleagues into our confidence and ask their permission to go.

As we expected there was no hesitation in their approval. They were perfectly in favour of the idea and willing to cope with the whole hospital even if no medical replacements arrived.

So Tony and I got down to detailed planning and accumulation of anything to help us on our way. There was a need for clothes, a rucksack each, sufficient food for two weeks, matches and a compass. I had already decided to accept the kind offer of keeping the page of the atlas. Clothes were not a great problem because many of the patients came in with old civilian clothes which were stored in lockers in the wards. The ward orderly could apply for new battle dress or Red Cross clothes from the Quartermaster's store and often got them. In this way I had accumulated a worse-for-wear waterproof jacket and a passable pair of brown trousers, socks, shoes, pullover and shirt of my own made an escaping outfit. We both had a rucksack and our store of food was mounting daily by saving from the rations and swapping cigarettes, which had an outstanding value, for Red Cross parcel food. Chocolate, cheese, biscuits, condensed milk, meat roll, were not hard to come by when tobacco or fags were available.

We had thought many times of our exit from the hospital and could find no better way than the route Dearlove had chosen. Practically all the hospital buildings and compound were surrounded by a double barbed wire fence. This in the middle of the town was difficult to approach. It was only the wall of the building on our side, which lined the street below, which was not enclosed. There were no windows on the road side of our building. We lived on the top floor with windows facing only into the compound of the hospital. Our window was at the west end and the other side of the west wall two storeys down was a one-storey building which abutted on to the road. The difficulty of getting to the road was walking along a narrow ledge where the slate roof of the smaller building joined our wall which we suspected was surfaced with rough plaster that was liable to crumble. There was no easy way of inspecting it apart from being lowered down to see. Dearlove had made some noise with falling plaster but had managed it and we were confident that we could do the same.

By early August we were ready to go and reckoned that sufficient time had elapsed for the guard to have lost their excessive vigilance since Dearlove had broken out. There was never any sign that they had any idea of the escape route. Had they suspected that he had been lowered from our window there would certainly have been a greater search and investigation and none of us had seen them taking any interest in the slate roof. The Quartermaster had visited us on several occasions since and had never again mentioned Dearlove. It was all very odd and there may have been something in my theory.

We got hold of some rope which was an undoubted improvement on sheets. We planned to leave on a night just after new moon when it would be small and give a minimum of light, sufficient to see the main objectives. All windows were blacked out which had the advantage of eliminating potential viewers. At 10.30 p.m. it was as dark as it would get. We tossed for going first and that lot fell on me.

There was a loop of a bowline knot at the end of the rope sufficiently large to take a foot and two simple knots higher up for gripping. With my left foot in the loop and holding hard I was lowered down to the level and it was then up to me to hook myself on to the lower wall with my right foot. At the corner there was fortunately sufficient standing space to make a complete turn while still holding on to the rope. Then with my back to the wall and my rucksack in front of my abdomen hanging from my neck I was able to stabilise myself and get ready for walking sideways along the ledge. I let go the rope with some trepidation. The plaster behind me was not exactly loose but little bits flaked off and made a noise which magnified unbelievably in that somewhat electric atmosphere. The fear of the plaster giving way behind was equal to the risk of slipping down on to the slates of the roof in front which sloped gradually down and away from the wall. At the other end of the ledge was the wall lining the road where the sentries patrolled round the hospital. This ledge spanning the width of the roof was about thirty feet long and as I got nearer to the road I could see that the wall was higher than the ledge which would give me hiding space while waiting for the sentry to pass.

It was a great relief to get to the other side and crouch down out of sight. Lying there my ears were cocked for two things, Tony coming round the corner on to the ledge and the step of the sentry on the cobbled road just below me. Within thirty seconds the unmistakable steps of the sentry passed by and five seconds later a scraping noise alerted me that Tony was turning the corner on to the ledge.

We had arranged to be independent of each other as regards dropping down into the road between the sentry patrols and to meet at a spot we both knew. It was a garage out of the town where the German doctor had taken his petrol at times when we were out with him.

A few more seconds and I calculated that the sentry had turned the corner and that it was time to go. Hanging from the wall at arms' length I first dropped my rucksack and then landed with as little commotion as possible. All went well. There was no shouting, no shooting, which gave Tony a clear pitch to do the same.

Within a quarter of an hour we were together behind the garage building. In sheer relief and excitement we hugged each other with such intensity and endearment that our behaviour, in ordinary society, would have been suspect. We were out of the cage for the first time in fourteen months and the feeling of freedom and exhilaration was immense. It was pure joy whilst it lasted.

After that period of emotional release our legs automatically took over and started a walk of 500 kilometres or more, but the thought of that was no problem. It was a means of trying our luck. The road to Hof was quiet and we made good progress. One lorry came along with dimmed lights and we dashed into the hedge while it passed. As we walked we could now give thought to our immediate plans. It was safe to presume that our absence in the hospital would not be discovered before 9 or 10 a.m. the next morning and by then we hoped to be out of the neighbourhood and well out of sight. It would be important to lie very low during daylight for the next few days. We were on the Hof road but had no accurate idea of the distance. The police there were certain to be alerted as soon as we were discovered missing. If at all possible it would be safer to get to the other side of Hof before the bell rang.

We were walking at a good rate and presuming Hof was no more than thirty kilometres it might be possible to get through the town during the early hours of daylight and hide up on the other side. It was all go and we felt in fighting trim.

Three kilometres or so back we had passed through a village without any trouble; there was no sign of life, it being then after midnight.

Now we came to another village, all was quiet until a dog barked and then another and the peace of the little place, at one in the morning, was alarmingly disturbed. It was a heartrending situation and there was nothing to do but forge ahead and hope that the inhabitants were used to that sort of disturbance.

We were practically through the village and the barking was dying down when suddenly a large figure loomed up and stood in front of us.

'Stop!' said a gruff and stern voice and a powerful torch shone on our faces.

'Who are you?' it demanded.

Tony's mind must have been working as quickly as mine. Was this the moment for physical attack, for bolting, or for trying to impress him with our purpose? After a second's rapid calculation we both came to the same conclusion, to stand and talk.

'We are slaters going to Hof to do roof repairs.'

'Where have you come from?'

'Poland.'

'No, where have you come from now?'

'From Schleiz.'

'What were you doing there?'

'Repairing a roof.'

Our challenger was a policeman of unusual size. He stood there in silence for a moment while he shone his torch down and pulled out a revolver.

'Show me your papers,' he demanded.

We stood there in silence, it was check mate and our mental computers were working at top speed. The chance of snatching his revolver, or of knocking him out, of running like hell in the dark with the hope of missing the bullets and having got away from him, the chance of not being caught later were all flicking through our minds at the speed of light. To go quietly would mean returning to square one, to attack a policeman would mean being shot if we were caught. Again the thousands and thousands of thinking cells in our grey matter came to the same decision.

'We have none.'

'No papers, why?'

'We have not been issued with any'. We were both answering,

sometimes in turn and sometimes together, depending with what speed we could muster sufficient German.

Holding his revolver in front of him the policeman came round behind us and put his hand into my rucksack and pulled something out.

'What have you here?' He shone his torch on it and then in a raucous shout said:

'*Was ist das*?'

It was a large slab of Cadbury's milk chocolate in all its purple and golden glory. It was the ace of trumps against our defence and at once had the effect of ending our case, but to the policeman, who had probably never seen anything quite like it before, it was a curio, but something unlikely to be found in a Polish worker's bag.

'You are prisoners of war?' he said.

'Yes.'

'Where from?'

'From the hospital in Schleiz.'

We were all in now. He stuck his revolver in Tony's back and marched us towards a house. He banged on the front door and banged again. A minute later a man in night clothes came to the door and all was explained. We were taken into a back room and told to sit down and the policeman took up his position on a chair near the door holding his revolver.

There we sat in abjection, our hopes blighted beyond all trace.

The policeman said nothing and was clearly occupied by the responsibility of his present charge.

Some time later the gentleman of the house appeared, fully dressed, he took the revolver and sat down by the door.

'If either of you move from your seat he will shoot.' said the policeman. 'You understand?'

We may have nodded.

'Do you understand?' he shouted.

There was a double 'yes' and he was satisfied. He left the room and we could hear him talking on a phone in the passage outside. 'Two French prisoners' I picked up out of the conversation and then no more until an obvious 'fifteen minutes' came through just at the end. I imagined he was talking to someone at our future destination and it seemed that he would be there in a quarter of an hour, about the time it would take to get to Schleiz.

The policeman came back and took over his revolver.

''*Raus*!' he shouted at us waving his weapon towards the door.

Outside in the road was an old car. We were waved into the back seats and the policeman took up his position beside the driver and sat turned round facing us with his revolver pointing first at one and then at the other. The gentleman of the house and presumably the owner of the car drove it with some trepidation, worried not only by the trouble in the back but also by a lack of confidence in the mechanism of the vehicle. Somewhere during the journey he pulled up, got out and lifted the bonnet. This was another opportunity for the policeman to repeat his warning about moving. There was a moment, while he was finding his torch for the driver, that he was off guard but the chance did not move either of us to take action. It was too difficult a starting point. It may have been the fan belt, the water or the oil that was worrying the driver because the engine was obviously too hot. The lid of the bonnet banged down and the driver returned to his seat. He was in no hurry to start which suggested some overheating trouble. We sat there for a time and once again our friend issued us another warning about moving. Then we were off and without any further hitch pulled up outside a building in Schleiz. It could be nothing else but the town gaol and we were soon seated in the locked reception room awaiting further developments.

Seated there, in a very dim light, in the sort of mood that we were in was not productive of conversation.

'They seem to think we are French,' said Tony after some minutes.

I agreed at once and it was interesting to know that he had caught the same bit of the conversation.

'Did you hear anything else?' I said.

'No, nothing very much.'

'There doesn't seem to be any need to disillusion them at present.'

That was all he said and half an hour later the door was unlocked and in came a gaoler.

'Come,' he said.

As we stooped to pick up our rucksacks he said, 'Leave your bags here.'

'Why?' I said.

'They have to be searched,' said the gaoler.

Reluctantly we left them and followed him down a passage and then climbed a spiral iron staircase to the second storey.

Here we were both put into the same room and the door

locked. It was still pitch-dark outside but a little light in the ceiling allowed us to see the main objects.

There was a wooden bunk on each side with a thin straw mattress. At the foot of the bunk was one thin blanket and a small pillow. There was no furniture but a shelf on the wall between the bunks was a place to put things and underneath was a pot. We were both soon asleep.

At some early hour we were wakened and issued with one slice of black bread and a cup of liquid bereft of any worthwhile taste. There was nothing to do after that but fortunately we had with us the prisoner's friend; a miniature pack of playing cards. I always slipped a pack into my trouser pocket whenever there were likely to be periods of frustrating boredom.

We were playing two-handed bridge when there was a clanging of keys and in came the gaoler.

'Get up, stand up,' he said. 'The colonel is coming.'

Through the door the sound of laboured steps coming up the spiral staircase indicated the seniority of the visitor. A sergeant in uniform came in first, stood upright and called us to attention, then turned round and saluted the colonel as he emerged from the top of the stairs. In came an old man with ruddy face and white hair. He wore full uniform, with medals and the rank of *Oberst*. Of medium height he had a bulging abdomen which was ill concealed by his tunic and the two carefully creased trouser legs hung in diminishing tubes from the expanse above and stopped a little too far from the ground. His expression was a mixture of pomposity, malevolence and bewilderment. He stood there recovering from the climb while his sergeant asked questions.

'You are prisoners of war?'

'Yes.'

'You have escaped from where?'

'Schleiz Hospital.'

'Where are your discs?'

These were square metal discs which we carried round our necks. To the escaping prisoner they were of great value, to allay the suspicion of spying and to establish identity. Once they were produced the sergeant showed no detailed interest in them and they were slipped back under our clothing.

'For this you will be punished,' he said.

The colonel turned round to the sergeant and said,

'Show them how to stand to attention.'

He demonstrated a position with the arms at the side and the knuckles forward. I did not change my position with the thumbs forward.

At that moment the colonel sprang into aggressive action, shouted out '*So*' and displayed his hand, knuckles forward by the side of his trouser leg. Then he lifted one leg and tried to kick my hand. It was a very undignified procedure and he nearly toppled over, but it was a perfect moment for us and Tony lost no time.

'In England we stand to attention like this,' he said, showing his thumb just behind the seam of his trousers.

'*Engländer*?' queried the colonel in a strained voice, turning towards the gaoler.

There was no reply.

'Who are you?' asked the sergeant.

'British officers,' I replied.

That was the end of the encounter. The party turned round, filtered out and there was a clang of keys in the lock. After that the shouting started. It was the colonel and we caught the words '*Französiche*' and '*Poilu*'. Doubtless both the sergeant and the gaoler were getting hell and would realise that the mistake they had made was something apart for a retired colonel of the Junker class.

The next day we left the civilian gaol with two guards for a destination, as usual, unknown, wondering, with many other queries, what form our punishment would take. Our rucksacks were returned with all closed tins removed but surprisingly enough the chocolate and biscuits and cheese were still intact.

In the evening we arrived at a camp and were allotted to a room with some twenty other men. It was Camp Stalag IXC, Bad Sulza. It soon became clear that we were there for a period of solitary confinement and that evening, spent with people in the know, was to prove of great value. We were told that the solitary confinement block was an isolated concrete building in the compound and that anyone in the camp could walk around the outside. There was one essential weapon, the end of a broken spoon handle, which we were each given. With this it was possible to turn the lock of the little window. At dusk, if a pebble hit the window, it should be opened immediately and with luck in would come some goodies.

At that time of year dusk was about eight o'clock and as everyone had to be in their huts by eight it was a delicate timing, just a few minutes before, provided the field was clear.

Next morning Tony and I had to report to the guard room. Here we were relieved of our rucksacks and had to empty and turn inside out all our pockets. We were left with nothing but our clothes but the broken spoon handle was in my shoe under the lining. We were taken to the block and locked in separate cells.

There was a little window up high with a simple metal bar across it. By standing on the bunk it was easy to reach it. The cell was eight foot by six, with a single wooden bunk and, like the civilian gaol, it had a thin straw mattress and one, very much worn, blanket. A shelf on the wall and a commode completed the amenities. We had been told that we had two weeks confinement. We knew that rations were a twice daily issue of two slices of black bread and water and so the outlook was potentially bleak and I sat on my bunk with my back to the wall thinking of the last thirty-six hours.

The door was unlocked and I was ordered to collect my bucket and cloth, fill it with water and to wash the floor of my room and the whole corridor. Presumably that was my chore as a new boy. There were ten cells and a corridor which ran the length of the building with a guard room next to the only outside door. At the other end of the corridor was a wash place with a sink with one cold tap, a sluice and a place for a row of buckets and cloths.

Washing the corridor was something new and was a useful introduction to a detailed study of the geography of the place. A few bumps against Tony's door made him lie on the floor and have a few whispering comments. We seemed to be the only inmates. At the other end of the corridor was the guard room and as I fiddled around there, slopping the cloth, the sentry was seated on a high stool.

'You are a doctor?' he said.

At that moment my thoughts were about six miles away, wondering how we could have avoided that village and the barking dogs and whether it would have been worth while bolting from the policeman. It was very dark and he would probably have missed, but the chances of getting out of the neighbourhood . . .

And then suddenly this odd question from the sentry brought me back. I glanced up from the floor at him sitting there, with a rather worried look on his face.

'Yes,' I said.

He then started to tell me all about his wife and that she was expecting her first baby very soon. He was obviously genuinely concerned about her welfare and particularly wanted to know more of the first signs of starting labour. Apparently they lived away from any town and it either meant her having the baby at home with little chance of help or getting transport and that was very difficult. He was worried that he would have to be the midwife and wanted to know the sort of things that would have to be done.

In my best possible German, which was third rate, I tried to explain to him the start of labour pains, the way they would develop and in what position his wife should lie. Many details followed including the umbilical cord and the afterbirth and what to do with the baby as soon as it was born. Many of the points had to be repeated and explained with complicated postures and hand movements. The floor cloth was a handy addition to the demonstration. A few more questions came out slowly after considerable thought and then he said, 'Thank you'.

I resumed my floor washing with great vigour and sense of purpose, knowing that the sentry and I had something very much in common. The bucket was emptied down the sluice, washed out and put in its correct place. I returned to my cell to lie down and try to get some sleep, but come it would not. There was nothing to do but to sit longitudinally along the bunk, resting against the wall. So this was solitary confinement. After fourteen months of prisoner of war life when one was never alone it was not at all unpleasant in its early stages. To let the mind idle and to do nothing physically but breathe was no hardship and hunger had not yet raised its ugly head.

During the early evening in came the second issue of two slices of black bread and a mug of water. It was a different sentry.

By half past seven I was ready at the window end of my bunk with my broken spoon handle; a trial turn had opened the lock without difficulty so that it was just a question of being ready at the moment of action.

It was possible to hear the other prisoners in the camp walking up and down outside and the activity had increased considerably during the last half hour or so, since they had returned to camp from work outside. Sure enough at about five minutes to eight there came a ping at the window. Up I jumped, turned the lock and pushed the window half open. A few seconds later in flew a bit of chocolate and a cigarette box. Nothing more, so I closed up. In the cigarette box were three cigarettes and some strikable matches. It was a great thrill to see the plan work and to have something to chew and smoke. There was a little peep-hole in the door so that the sentry could see what was going on inside but at night, with so little noise, it was possible to hear him as soon as he left his room and prepared for his inspection. It was safe to have a cigarette and the piece of chocolate helped me to settle at about midnight to try and get some sleep.

Nothing happened out of routine until the next evening when there was a repeat and in came more chocolate, some biscuits and more cigarettes.

On the third morning at about six-thirty the door opened. It was the sentry whose wife was to have a baby. He had had a day off. To my astonishment he slipped me a parcel and said it was a present from his wife. He put his finger to his lips, indicating that no one must know and out he went, locking the door, as quickly as he had come in.

It was a sponge cake, with a layer of jam, sufficiently large to give about ten good sized slices, and sitting there looking at it I found it almost impossible to believe. It was a most astounding turn up and gave an unmistakable feeling of well being around the stomach and indeed everywhere. There was nothing to cut it with which seemed a pity. He surely would think of this because it seemed such a shame to break it into rough pieces. The handle of the spoon would help but it would be unwise to use it lest his confidence be jolted.

After release from the washing of the corridor I gathered up courage to ask him for a knife to cut it. In my room, with a pen-knife, he cut up the whole cake into about twelve pieces. I had had nothing like that since capture and still marvel because it took the edge off the whole stay in confinement. A surprising amenity was an issue of literature from the library, a battle which had apparently been won by the British Medical Officer of the Camp to permit books in solitary confinement. So with a sponge cake, Walpole's *Rogue Herries* series to read and chocolate and cigarettes coming in through the window, solitary confinement — for me — was a picnic.

Three weeks later Tony and I were packed off with two guards and I realise now how lucky we had been to go to Bad Sulza where they were obviously not geared up for coping with escapees. It was a camp for other ranks working on the land. Why we were not sent to the Officers' *Strafelager*, Oflag IVC, commonly known as Colditz, which was in the neighbourhood, was a mystery and indeed a fortunate administrative error.

By the evening we were back in Spangenberg and glad to be

taken to the lower camp, Elbersdorf. It was my old haunt which I had left on 17th February, some six months ago. Of the two camps at Spangenberg, this was the preferable. It was by the river in the middle of the village which provided some outside focus of interest. The other was in a château on the top of a wooded hill surrounded by a moat and very remote from any habitation.

That first evening, having just got into bed after a tiring day of very frustrating and mediocre train travel, the door of our room opened and in came someone with a piece of paper in his hand. There was immediate silence. It was the British evening news bulletin and someone explained to me that there was now a wireless set in the camp and that it was used for the evening news only, which was taken down in shorthand and brought to each room by a reporter every evening. It was a fantastic addition to camp life and the next day the origin of the service came home with a bump.

I ran into Dicky, one of the medical officers who had brought the remaining wounded of the 51st Division up to the hospital in Germany.

'Did you hear the news last night?' he asked. 'Yes, what a wonderful service,' I replied.

'Do you remember?'

And then in a flash the penny dropped. It was he who had arrived from France carrying a portable wireless which looked like a little attaché case. He knew that he was going to Spangenberg and I had strongly advised him not to take it.

'You remember, you said I was crazy to try?' I nodded and my head went very low. Then as the whole story came out I cashed in on the glory of it and took an inverted pride in the fact that I had been proved so wrong.

At the time we came to the camp an escape tunnel was already planned and the first step taken. A well was to be excavated under the shower room floor, and a tunnel dug leading into it. By now the well had already been dug. I was asked to volunteer for digging duties and, realising that I had the status of a new boy, I could find no ready excuse for refusing. The worst shift was in the early morning, before breakfast. It meant getting up before six and dropping down a cold wet hole with water at the bottom of the well which had first to be baled out. The initial few minutes on the face were unpleasant, but soon, as one got warmed up, the itch to dig grew. The object of each shift was to dig sufficient to fill about thirty boxes. This was about as much as the carriers and receivers at the other end could cope with. During an average day the tunnel would advance somewhere between one and two feet. After each digging shift bed boards were wedged in to shore up the roof and sides.

As the face got nearer to the sentry's path greater latitude was given to the cessation of activity. The digger lay still while the light was out and could hear the tread of the boots pass over above.

The escape committee had made careful selection of those to try their luck. Selection depended on many factors, of which speaking German and potential value at home were not without priority. The first two or three out were bound to have a better chance than those following. A few would be lucky enough to have papers forged by the hand of John Mansel. An architect in pre-war days, he had dedicated his life in camp and his outstanding artistic ability to helping his fellow prisoners in this way. Freely and very delicately painted, John Mansel could produce a pass signed by the Commandant quite indistinguishable by the inexpert observer.

As the tunnel got near to its finishing stage the earth above and under the dining room was giving considerable concern to those in the know but few realised that every time they sat down to eat there were 40 tons of earth the other side of the ceiling.

Then in October, just before the tunnel was planned to surface, a few *grands blessés* and some doctors were told, quite suddenly, that they were being transferred for repatriation.

It seemed quite unbelievable but potentially a more certain and comfortable method of getting home than crawling out of the tunnel.

Grands blessés, doctors and RAMC personnel were gathered together from camps all over Germany into a *Heimatlager* (Repatriation camp) which was virtually a series of barns in a field, but who bothered about conditions under those prospects?

Two trains took us west and when we got into France our confidence started to mount to the extent of throwing all our food reserves out to the waving onlookers. Near Rouen word seemed to have got around and there were many out to see us go by.

That night we were housed in a school in Rouen, carefully prepared by nuns to give us a feeling of welcome. There were all sorts of rumours about going home. Some had heard that the boat was lying in Rouen Dock, others that we were going from Dieppe to Folkestone.

One day slipped to another and nothing happened and then the news filtered through that the whole move was off. It was desperate for all of us but worse for the wounded and ill who had been moved all the way from Germany with such high hopes. The bed cases returned by train to Germany and the rest of us, the majority of them permanently unfit, together with doctors, padres and RAMC personnel, were moved to an old British transit camp on the race course at Sotteville, over the river from Rouen.

There were 1,300 of us. The accommodation was in old Nissen Huts without flooring and with the winter coming on the prospect was bleak but so long as we remained in France repatriation was possible.

It seemed that the exchange had fallen through at the last moment. The German prisoners in Britain had actually boarded the boat in Folkestone but the German High Command suddenly decided to refuse to take part in a numerically uneven interchange. At that time of the war the difference was very considerable.

The final nail in the coffin of repatriation for most of us came on 19th December 1941 when one thousand were moved back to Germany and Poland. Three hundred were left as a token of good will, as it were, in the event of repatriation negotiations being renewed.

In the Sotteville camp was a hospital bungalow building. It housed the major disabled, the temporary sick and officers on duty for the camp such as the senior officer, medical officers and the quartermaster, Jock Finlayson. He and I were friends of long standing, we had been in sister casualty clearing stations since their formation in Leighton Buzzard in September 1939. He was in charge of the kitchen and was responsible for receiving and distributing all rations from the Germans. He came into contact with them more than anyone else and kept his ear close to the ground. There was no news of any sort about repatriation but by mid-January Jock was fairly convinced that a move was coming in the future and that almost certainly it would be east. He told me of this hunch one evening with an inviting look in his eye. From then on we got thinking. It seemed crazy to go back to Germany.

In the early days in this camp a few had got through a single barbed wire fence but had never been ambitious enough to get further than the town except for one officer who was with them. He had never returned and as far as we knew might be on his way home. The rest, after a good booze-up, had all been recaptured and brought back. Since then the compound had been very much reduced in size and the barbed wire and sentries increased to bring it up to full anti-escape level.

The more we talked about it the more determined we became to get away. It was not going to be easy. Getting out of the camp meant one of three methods, through or over the barbed wire at night, tunnelling under it or passing through the main and only gate, hidden in rubbish or in a vehicle or in disguise. There was no time for tunnelling, getting through or over the barbed wire was now very difficult and only a miracle would get us both through the main gate as Jock was so well known by the Germans and he was with them all the time while in the kitchen. A last moment jump on to a leaving vehicle could never include both of us because I was never allowed in the kitchen premises and the drive from there to the main gate was through open ground.

A much better method grew on us slowly; to hide in the camp when they moved away. We decided to start digging a space under the floor sufficiently large to accommodate us both.

In the hospital building, where we both lived, was a small room, originally a side ward with a single bed but more recently used as a reading room for anyone who wanted to be quiet. It had a large sofa made out of odd bits of wood, sacking and padded with stuffing from Red Cross parcels. There was a large iron coke stove. The wooden floor on which it stood was protected by a square iron plate. From the top of the stove a black pipe, turning two right angles, went upwards to penetrate the ceiling.

During the night when the stove was out or almost so, and everyone in bed, we decided to have a look at this site. The stove and chimney were disconnected and moved to the side. The square of iron was lifted and underneath were floorboards, continuous but for one which had a join and both ends were nailed to a beam below. One end was prized up and a penetrating hand and forearm felt earth about a foot down. Everything was replaced and we sat on the sofa to think.

The floorboards were supported on joists and these probably ran from one wall to another or were supported in the interval by something else. The space between the floor and the earth of about one foot would be valuable for breathing and a good start, as it were, to our excavations. Enough earth would have to be removed to give room for us to lie side by side and sufficient height to sit up.

It was decided to cut the boards during the next night to make a hole sufficiently large to get through. Jock had access to the carpenter's workshop which was a considerable asset; without tools it would have been impossible.

Further cutting showed a joist obstructing entry if the iron plate was to fit back on to the permanently marked square on the boards. Cutting the joist meant that both ends had to have vertical supports from the ground and these would have to come between us as we lay.

A torch showed how the joists were supported by little brick walls, two layers of brick above the earth level. The good news was that there was sufficient ground space between the walls to take both of us lying down side by side and that the air space below the floor was extensive. We closed up and again sat on the sofa and discussed procedure.

Jock came up with the information that the camp was almost certainly moving about 14th February, judging by the longer term rations that had just been issued. This gave us two clear weeks to get our lair in working order. Getting rid of the earth was going to be a real problem. Towards the end of the digging, when the holes were sufficiently big enough to get in, some earth could be disposed of down the air space but a lot of excavating had to be done before either of us could get under the floor.

The answer was to start some fresh digging in the compound and Jock decided that he would have a kitchen garden for the spring and would get two of his staff to do a bit each day. It was a bright idea which presented a naive, optimistic face to the goons.

Every late evening and night we took it in turns to dig and dispose of earth. With a freshly dug garden this was easy, but during the second week it turned very cold and snowed a lot, but Jock insisted that his men should continue to dig a bit each day. It was extraordinary that none of the goons tumbled to what was happening.

The plan was now definitely on and traditionally should have been reported to an escape committee but there was none. I told the Senior British Officer, Colonel Harvey, and he approved after some explanation but rather gave the impression that he thought the idea over-optimistic.

The building had a long central corridor with rooms on either side, some sleeping five or six, others two or three and the rest were single. There were about thirty people in all living there and it was not long before they all knew what was going on, but they went their ways and took no notice of our odd activities. The best time to work was after 10 p.m. when most, except for a bridge party or two, had turned in and there were no goons in the camp. Apart from a torch under the floor it was possible to work without any light in the building and to get rid of the earth outside.

Getting the two halves of the lair sufficiently deep to permit sitting up and long enough to lie down was a formidable target and by Thursday it became glaringly obvious, with only two nights left, that the project was going to be unfinished. We were both very short of sleep and had allowed for a good night's rest in our own beds on Saturday night before taking the plunge.

Somebody had to be found to replace the boards, iron plate, stove and chimney after we were down. George Hadley, who lived in the building and was an old friend and the medical specialist to Jock's unit, kindly volunteered to do all this early on Saturday morning. We had a rehearsal one evening and decided that a crowbar would be necessary for getting out again. Something suitable was found in the kitchen stores and placed under the floor, but we never had a proper rehearsal for getting out, which proved to be a bad mistake.

All Friday evening and night we worked like demons and by dawn on Saturday, utterly exhausted, we decided to call it a day, and turned in for two hours. All day Jock was busy with the packing up in the kitchen stores and I with helping getting everyone ready for the journey. It was now universal knowledge that the camp was to be moved on Sunday morning. The destination was not known but the direction would undoubtedly be east, back to Germany or Poland.

The last evening was spent in collecting all the things that were to go down with us but the next step should have been a meticulous placing of all the articles so that in the morning there was nothing to do but get out of bed and jump straight down the hole to await the closing down procedure by George Hadley.

Things did not work out like that. It was the last evening for everyone and there was an undoubted feeling of get together throughout the camp. Not that there was any cause for celebration, but drink had got through the barbed wire in exchange for chocolate and cigarettes and what more appropriate occasion to finish it up.

Our building filled up with many friends and the reading room was continually occupied. It was impossible to open up the hole and Jock and I very unwisely got involved in the spirit of pseudo celebration. So the tension of the last two weeks and the thought of the next day melted into mutual goodwill. Our endeavour was toasted and many wished us good luck but the element of envy was not apparent. Go to bed they would not and so we both turned in by midnight determined to have one night's sleep.

CHAPTER FOUR

Out and About

And so we both turned in that Saturday night, inadequately prepared because our friends were determined to celebrate into the early hours. Jock was quite certain, being an old soldier, that he would wake early, long before the German doctor arrived. I had put my kit and clothes ready, got into bed and was asleep instantaneously.

The night passed. The next thing I remember was a violent shaking of my shoulder and collecting my thoughts realised that things were not quite right.

'Wake up, Pip, the Jerry doctor is here.'

'Why, what's the time?'

'Nearly eight o'clock.'

This was a fine mess to be in and visions of the whole plan collapsing dawned on me fairly rapidly. The after effects of the last night still prevented a swift decision but one thing was clear, it was essential that the doctor should not see me.

'What's happened to Jock?'

'He's still in bed.'

'Has anyone kicked him?'

'Yes, he's in about the same state as you!'

'Gosh, what a mess. Where is the doctor now?'

'He's gone to see the Colonel. If you get across the corridor now he may not see you.'

I gathered up my clothes, two rugs, two Red Cross parcels and a pack of things, opened the door gingerly and looked up and down the corridor. There was no one to be seen. I nipped across to the door of the reading room and quickly closed it. The chimney and stove had to be moved and the hole opened up. Everything was chucked down in a heap and the lid put over the gap while I sat on the sofa to await Jock.

It seemed ages. The door opened suddenly and in came Jock, looking pale and dazed but with an impish grin around the corners of his mouth and eyes.

'That was a close one. The Jerry has just gone into his room. I thought he would visit our room first, he generally does, but for some lucky reason he didn't today.'

'Whatever made you oversleep this morning of all times?'

'I don't dare to think. I never had a better night's sleep in all my life.'

'Nor have I, it doesn't bear investigation. I thought I should be awake most of the night.'

'Anyway let's get cracking.'

Jock dropped his stuff down the hole and now we had to decide who took which side. It was a toss and Jock lost, so he got down first. Just then the door opened and George came hurriedly in.

'Hurry up, you bastards, the doctor will be wanting one of you in a minute.'

I got down to my side and George immediately started replacing the boards in their correct position. The sheet of iron, gently though it was done and doubtless making little noise outside, seemed to be put down with a bang. Then with much rattling and grinding and banging the stove was put into position and then the noise of the chimney piping being adjusted concluded the manoeuvre. There was a pause for a moment while doubtless a check was being made to see that everything looked normal and undisturbed. The sofa was moved a little and then George's voice, close by the floor:

'It's all OK now – cheerio – best of luck.'

The door opened and closed and he was gone.

We sat in silence. An air of finality and impending destiny pervaded us both. The switch had been thrown and there was no going back. Ten minutes previously we had been in bed. Suddenly wakened we had worked quickly and automatically and had had no time to think or consider the wisdom of going ahead. It was probably just as well. Once the doctor had seen either of us it would have been all over and the efforts of the persuasion party who were going to build up the story of us departing during the night, unless they could be stopped, would be a danger to themselves. We should have been in position by seven o'clock and luck had certainly been with us in avoiding disaster at the very outset of our project.

The reaction set in. Cramped in our hole side by side with nothing to do but wait, Jock's thoughts must have wandered in much the same direction as mine. Now that the lid had gone down, the boards fixed and the stove set in position, the die had been cast and we were no longer one of the camp, no longer among friends of so many months living together. Our present and our future lay in this burrow in the earth and our status would be that of hunted rabbits until we saw fit to get out.

The hole had two berths, one each side of two shoring up poles. There was sufficient room to half lie and half sit as for reading in bed, but a further attempt to sit up was limited by the floorboards and lying down was only possible with the knees well bent. Jock had lost the toss which meant that he was on the side away from the exit hole which gave the slight advantage, when sitting right forward, of making space to stretch the neck. Lying close to the shoring poles on one side gave a sufficient gap on the other for the arm to go down to the side and there was a space laterally at head level of about nine inches between the floor beams and the ground extending to the bricks supporting the rafters.

The clothes, blankets, food and other paraphernalia were still beneath us where they had been chucked in haste and it was going to take a lot of careful manoeuvring to get everything correctly placed. This was fortunate, it gave us something to do while waiting for the balloon to go up. Gradually, little by little, we got things sorted out. Everything was brought round to our tummies and then stored laterally in the air space between the joists and the ground. The rugs were slowly worked round underneath our heads, backs, buttocks and legs and once in place were a welcome comfort and foundation of our well-being. We were still in our pyjamas which made excellent underwear and over these went other clothes, keeping the trousers and mackintosh folded away to maintain some degree of sartorial standard for the time of exit.

Meanwhile there were noises of increasing activity, the sound of hobnailed boots scraping on the tiled corridor and to our envy we could hear the clatter of knives and forks and plates as our room mates sat just above us having their breakfast, the last meal in the camp. Orders were being shouted and the harsher, firmer sound of Jerry boots resounded throughout the building. Mingled with this there was much whistling and disjointed singing, revealing the elation of men on the move after months of stagnation and boredom regardless of the prospect.

There was hammering and banging as pictures and shelves were torn from the walls. Hurried footsteps resounded to a crescendo over our heads, doors banged and the scraping of beds, tables and chairs seemed interminable. Pieces of conversation filtered through and the laughter from *ad hoc* groups, which had time to snatch humour in response to the general drive and hustle of the Jerry guards, was all part of the prisoner of war requittal. It was queer to be completely detached and yet so close to this bustle of activity of which we had been part for so long and sobering to know that it was soon to leave us to our own devices. We might have been buried alive as indeed we were.

We began to long for them to go but it seemed that they never would. Until their departure we should not know what the next stage had in store. It must have been about two hours later, to us days might have passed, before a raucous voice shouted, '*Alles aus, alles aus*', followed by the inevitable '*Heraus, 'raus, 'raus*!'

The noise of feverish activity gradually subsided and one by one or two by two feet slowly and purposefully sauntered down the corridor for the last time. Then when everyone would seem to have gone the door into the little room above us was opened quickly. George's voice said, 'We're going now, chaps – all the best.' We heard his footsteps down the passage and a door bang as he left the building.

Now there was silence. It was almost complete except for some shouting far away in the distance. They must be going on parade, we thought, about 300 of them and soon the guard would be busy counting and adding up the figures. There would be some anxious but amusing moments for the few who knew of our whereabouts as the deficient count slowly clicked from possible arithmetical error to factual truth. It must have been a much more anxious moment for the Commandant. Jock had heard from his German contacts in the kitchen that he had been given definite orders that the move was to be carried out without the possibility of any escapes. To the Germans an escape in occupied and potentially friendly country near to the coast and the west wall was far more menacing than in their own country.

We lay still and anxious during what we knew was the lull before the storm. We spoke little and then in only very low whispers. We were apprehensive as to when and how the storm would break. It already seemed hours since George had bid us farewell.

When it started my heart missed a beat and then raced until it seemed that the pulse in my neck would be heard outside the building. Two or three guards, half walking, half running, entered the building, threw open the doors and made a quick search of all the rooms. This did not take long and apparently satisfied that they had fulfilled orders, they left the building. There was silence again except for the fading throb in my neck and temples.

It was only the herald, the storm was to come later.

There was nothing to say, not even in a whisper, we lay with our heads and necks propped against the wall of our den, steeped in foreboding and apprehension, our ears cocked like those of a hare, our palms cold and clammy and our eyes ever searching through the impenetrable darkness. The quietness and stillness exposed our hearing to excessive expectancy. The fall of a small pebble or a few grains of sand from the roof would sound like a thunderbolt on the keyboard of our senses. While peace lasted naively we built up a little hope that the search was over.

With a tremendous clatter the boots came back again, ten, twenty of them. Orders were shouted and tempers ran high. This was it, now the tempest would rage and beat and test the weaker spots. Chairs and tables were overturned, cupboards pulled from the wall, casters of beds squeaked and squealed across the floor as the thud of heavy feet fluctuated from one room to another. They flung open the door of our room and stood within a foot of our heads. The sofa which had been carefully constructed from odd bits of wood and stuffing from Red Cross parcels was turned upside down and ripped open. They may have inspected the floor as they stood round, one describing to the others what the room was used for and another giving a description of the two who were missing. As they talked they stamped like horses in a stable, the nails in their boots vibrating on the sheet of metal and dust trickled down between the boards. It was difficult to breathe without seeming to make some noise and the dread of coughing was intense. Nature never intended one to sit still and quiet during times of stress. The instinct is for action but here the slightest noise or smallest jerk which caused anything to fall or the earth from the walls to give way was perilous. The thumping pulse, the desire to breathe deeply seemed unduly prominent and the more the urge to cough was suppressed the greater became the tickle in the throat. One stifled cough would be disastrous.

The conversation ceased and gradually they left the building, presumably to search other huts in the camp. Not until all noise had died away for some time did I dare to clear my throat, lest someone might be lurking silently, listening for a noise.

Jock conveyed no evidence of these discomforts and fears, perhaps he was less sensitive or maybe, being an old soldier, he had learnt to control them.

My bag contained a box of tablets which had been taken from the medical treatment room on the previous day. In it were luminal, useful for over-excitement and the effects of stress, and opium, medically for the relief of pain but in our case for suppressing the desire to cough and the natural excretory functions.

We both had a tablet of each and the effect was excellent. Within a quarter of an hour there was a feeling of resignation and slowly we passed into a state of semi-stupor.

Time after time throughout the rest of the day guards returned for further searching and to get any available fresh evidence or merely to give, presumably, the officer in charge of the search the impression that they were doing the job thoroughly. During the afternoon a fresh group came back and entered the room on the opposite side of the corridor, the room where I had slept with four others. It was obvious that there was some new plan afoot by the business-like way in which they all walked into one room and dropped a heavy bundle which clanked. It sounded like a bag of tools. Some hammering was followed by a horrific, blood-curdling, rending sound, a noise which but for the tablets would have made my hair stand upright with fright. They were ripping up the floor-boards. We were wide awake now, our minds racing with suspense. Would they be content with that room or would they come to our little room and start the same thing there, moving the stove and the metal plate and then finding the cut boards underneath, proceed with excitement and sadistic vigour?

There was much to ponder about and plenty to imagine but one thing was obvious, to shout out as soon as the metal plate was removed before the crowbar penetrated our skulls. The idea of sheepishly crawling out of the hole among a group of excited and revengeful *deutsche Soldaten* gave no cause for pleasure and became increasingly hideous the more it was contemplated. Some days previously I remembered the German doctor had come into our room, where they were now working, suddenly and caught me feeling between the boards with a knife. He said nothing and pretended not to have noticed but it was an awkward moment and as my glance caught his it was obvious that the incident had been registered indelibly. This could well be the reason for attacking the floor, starting with that room. It was a little relief to think that they might abandon their project having drawn a blank in the bedrooms.

By bending forward and getting my head into the exit hole I was able to see through a small slit the light from the window. It was now getting dark and the luminous hands of my wristwatch showed a quarter past four. We had been thus closeted for over eight hours and although there had been plenty of distraction to relieve the boredom as it were it did indeed seem an age.

We lay still like a couple of mummies, our arms by our sides and our ears cocked to interpret the changes in the terrifying noise which kept us in a cold sweat. Then quite quickly it stopped and we heard them leave the room and come down the corridor. This was a terrible moment, was it our turn now or were they leaving the building? The tread of the boots came nearer and to our relief passed our door. They left the building and once again silence reigned. I had listened intently for the clank of a bag of tools but could not be satisfied that it had gone with them.

Jock whispered, 'That was a pretty close one.' There seemed nothing to add to that but it was a great relief to hear him after so long. We had lain so still for hours in complete silence and it was a happy change to have a little conversation, to move the legs and to ease the pressure on the bottom which was numb and indented by the pebbles beneath. Always our ears were alert.

The building was surrounded by grass covered with snow so that the approach of a visitor was inaudible until a footfall on the stone step outside the front door sounded the alarm, and off would go our hearts, thumping away behind our ribs.

As the evening drew on our building became entirely deserted and we were able to talk and move about in a very limited way. We decided to have more tablets and try to get some sleep with the idea of waking in the middle of the night for refreshment.

We sank into a welcome sleep and knew no more for many hours. What went on during that time we were never to know but nothing mattered very much as our hide-out was still intact.

Awaking I found Jock busy adjusting his rug. There had been a fall of earth from his wall and it had made him very uncomfortable. He was disposing of the debris into the air space, a handful at a time. It must have been this disturbance that woke me up. I looked at my watch. To my surprise it was 2.30 a.m. I told Jock and we agreed that now was the time for some food, we had been asleep for over six hours. The quiet was absolute and it was reasonable to suppose that anyone remaining in the camp was fast asleep. For a moment we contemplated getting out of the hole and leaving straightaway but immediately thought better of it.

Jock was in good form and ready for a meal and our thoughts both simultaneously turned to the steak and kidney pudding which rested in a tin at our feet. We made our beds as comfortable as possible and got out the little spirit stove and set it between the shoring poles. One match lit the stove and a candle and then with the tin opened and set over the flame we were definitely in business.

We lay back with reassuring contemplation of the things to come. The candle, after being so long without light, burnt like a fireball, illuminating our cavern with a golden hue. Jock ferreted about among the things at our feet and produced two cardboard plates and two spoons.

Never had a steak and kidney pudding been disposed of with such relish combined with the satisfaction of having achieved its preparation. It was beautifully hot with large lumps of steak and plenty of kidney and rich gravy. It had come from an American Red Cross parcel. This was followed by a thick slice of Dundee cake smothered in almonds from the same source. The meal was finished with half a slab of milk chocolate. Although we had not eaten for over thirty hours my appetite was not great but the meal was superb and tinged perhaps with an element of celebration of having got through the first day. We had a comfortable feeling that at our feet in two Red Cross boxes was enough food to keep us going for a week. We managed to make a cup of tea and that combined with a cigarette put the finishing touch to a feeling of well-being and rising morale which spread throughout our lair. The place was surprisingly warm and it needed no bug to know what it was to be snug in a rug. As a postprandial entertainment Jock produced a pocket chess set and got me check-mated in a surprisingly short time, and after three games it became very obvious that he was either better at chess or more able to cope with unusual circumstances.

About 5 a.m. we decided to settle down. The tablets had proved a great success so we took some more hoping to wake when activities started the next morning. The candle was blown out and very soon we knew no more.

In the morning we surfaced to the noise of a lot of feet and some shouting. All the rooms seemed to be entered and some furniture was moved about but there was no more wrenching of the floorboards much to our relief.

The party cleared off after a quarter of an hour or more and left the place all quiet. It seemed most likely that they had returned for a morning inspection to see if anything had changed during the night and to note any fresh evidence of our presence. It made us realise how unwise it would have been to try and get out of our hole that night as these guards had obviously slept in the camp. Originally we had hoped that they would leave with the prisoners. We decided to repeat the tablets and as a result were half asleep most of the morning until I was alerted about midday. A single person came into the building and entered the room next door on the same side of the corridor. I heard him set down a chair on the other side of the wall; it must have been about eight to ten feet away. Jock was still asleep. I wanted to tell him but did not dare to rouse him lest he wake up with a snort and start to talk before I could warn him. I lay rigidly still dreading that either of us would make a sound. The intruder remained quite quiet and still for some time and then I heard him move his chair and set something on the floor and I remember wondering if it was a listening apparatus.

Sleep must have come again until I was awakened some two hours later by the man pushing his chair and walking out of the building. The thought of him sitting there within a few yards of us fast asleep made me sweat a little. Thank God for the opium tablets. A single snore or cough would have been the end.

In the early hours we revived again. There was no sound and the crack in the boards showed no light. The time was 1.30 a.m. so that anyone in the camp should be fast asleep and it was a suitable opportunity to repeat the festivities of the night before. The candle beamed out like a light house and our cavern seemed to grow larger with acquaintance. The walls sparkled with little crystals amongst the pebbles and the earth. The spirit stove was set up between the poles and lit and very soon we were again relishing a succulent steak and kidney pudding. There was a feeling of less tension because we had got through another day and felt that the search was over and that probably even now the camp was deserted. It was replaced by an uneasy urge to get going, an impatience and restlessness to be under way. We knew that impatience had been the downfall of many an escapee and a decision, undoubtedly led by Jock, a little older and wiser, was made to remain another day. It was then about 2.30 a.m., too late to go. When the break did come it would be best to get going just after dark so as to cover as much distance as possible before dawn.

We knew that the camp was situated in a flask-shaped piece of land, a peninsula bounded by a loop of the Seine and connected to the open country by a narrow isthmus. We were at the bottom of the flask, close to the bridges across the Seine into Rouen which would all be controlled and hopeless to cross at night especially after the curfew. The peninsula was fifteen kilometres long, with a neck about three kilometres wide through which passed two important roads and some smaller lanes. Almost certainly there would be a control on the two main roads. It was our intention to get through the isthmus on the land between the roads before dawn. In the country beyond was the Fôret de la Londe and this would make good hiding ground for the next day and cover up our tracks.

Once out of the camp it would mean a distance of about thirteen kilometres. On the road this would be nothing more than a three-hour walk but across unknown country in the dark, scrambling through hedges and jumping ditches could be a very time-consuming journey. It needed little reflection to realise that it was much too late to start that night. This we discussed in a very quiet whisper and the unavoidable decision killed the urge to go and left a feeling of purposeful relaxation.

Our hole was cosy and warm and this was the hour that one had longed for all day. Having eaten well before our discussion, a hot sweet cup of tea and a cigarette expressed our mood of enforced idleness and contemplation. To lie back, pull at a fag, blow out the smoke and watch it drift slowly along the beam of our roof towards the exit hole where it found a way out between the boards got me to rehearsing mentally operation exit. Having won the toss for the best side, it was my responsibility to make the way open and get out first. Instinctively I put my right hand down to my side where the crowbar lay. With that the boards had to be levered loose sufficiently to get a purchase on the square plate of iron. This had to be levered little by little to the side until three of the boards could be removed, leaving a gap which by rehearsal was sufficiently wide to get through. This had been rehearsed but not the manoeuvre of loosening the boards and moving the metal plate. The reading room had been so often occupied that every moment we could gain entry was used for digging and earth removal so that the preliminary trial of getting out, which now seemed essential, was never put to test.

Great care would have to be taken not to knock the stove over in the process. This with the angled chimney piping, if it fell, would make a noise to be heard all over the camp. George had fixed the boards with short nails just sufficiently long to give a hold and they should not present a great difficulty. The first board could be raised slightly and levered back over its mate towards the wall. This would be followed by leverage of the iron plate away from the wall so as to free the second board and so on. It should be quite possible but I wasn't certain. It seemed crazy now not to have tried it out before.

Jock produced the chess set and my thoughts were switched to other things but not sufficiently to give me any chance of revenge for the previous night. After one game I gave up and told Jock where my mind was and we chatted about the technique in detail, but situated where he was there was little that he could do to help, space was far too limited to allow him to get underneath until I had got out. I was itching to get going, so in a mood of frustration I took some more tablets and left Jock to blow out the candle. As I lay waiting for the tablets to take effect my thoughts turned to home. After two days we were still no nearer; how far it seemed to that sceptred isle set in a silver sea.

In the morning we were awakened. There were footsteps coming again down the corridor and our hearts sank. Depression descended on us acutely and I felt that I could stand no more searching and shouting. Would this hunt never end? Had they not satisfied themselves yet that we had truly gone the night before the move? How long it seemed since George had bid us farewell and his footsteps had echoed down the corridor, the last friendly noise that we had heard. Had they told the guard of our escape and shown them the place in the barbed wire where we had got over or had they forgotten or not forced the opportunity? Surely the guard must think by this time that we were away?

The footsteps were busy in the room opposite doing something to the floor and pulling things about. What hope was there now that our floor would not be pulled up? It seemed such an obvious thing to do. Fading were our dreams of the night before that the search was over and that we should soon be out. I was tired, so tired of lying still and listening, always listening. My ears ached with it and my eyes from staring at darkness. Would we never see light again before we had turned white like sauerkraut?

What could they be doing? They seemed different, no shouting, no stamping, no heavy boots. They sauntered from one place to another, laughing and talking. Then an idea struck us. They were new troops moving in to be billeted in the camp. The search had been abandoned and here were a different unit moving in to prepare their barracks. Soon they would be in the little room over our heads, perhaps lying on the floor over our hole, smoking, joking and showing each other photographs of their wives and kids.

What an outlook, what hopelessness descended on us. This was a possibility that had never come into our calculations. There seemed no way out but to give ourselves up. We lay still, stunned with rejection and remorse.

The door into our little room clicked open and in sauntered a pair of feet. They stopped as if the owner were surveying the room and then shuffled around just above our heads and stood still again. It was quite definitely the noise of slippers and I thought of patients moving into a temporary hospital. They shuffled again and then the person sat down on the couch and bounced up and down.

'*Ici une bonne couchée*!' It was a female voice.

'French cleaners' Jock said, very close to my ear. Another came in to try it and they bounced together and giggled unrestrainedly. We could have laughed, laughed out of sheer joy. What relief there was in that moment was beyond description. Our hearts went out to them, these *belles francaises*. The desire to burst out from our hole and wring them by the hands and kiss and dance, or even just to shout to them, was intense. '*Nous sommes anglais, vos amis*' was on my lips but they were sealed.

Instead we lay relaxed and smiling, listening to their idle chatter, pleasant repartee and laughter.

'*Ou, la la, j'ai trouvé une boite de confiture.*'

'*Les prisoniers anglais, ils ont tous mon vieux*.'

All the morning they moved their pails about, shook their brooms, opened and shut windows and banged the skirting as they swept the corners. Always they shuffled in their slippers. At midday they departed and never returned but unknown to them they were the harbingers of great news and left behind them two happy, devoted admirers.

It was now clear that this evening was the time to break, with the cleaning over, new troops were to be expected and we prayed that it would not be before tomorrow. No one entered the building that afternoon, but out of habit we lay with our ears cocked and conscious always of the possible intrusion of a tip-toeing listener but none came. We were itching now to be under way as soon as it was dark. At about 4 p.m. we started to get ready, selecting the food to take. This was to be packed round inside our shirts once our trousers were on and the belt tightened. There was much more than we could manage which seemed a pity but we were determined not to carry a bag or haversack. It had been my undoing previously.

We ate our fill and finished the meal with a large piece of chocolate, lumps of sugar and a cigarette. The streak of light had now almost disappeared. We squirmed and wrestled to get our trousers on and tighten our belts and then lay still for a moment, listening once more. There was not a sound. It was time to go. I got hold of the crowbar and gently inserted it under the first board and with a little squeaking, wrenched it out with no difficulty. The same was repeated at the other end and the board then levered backwards over the others towards the wall. There was now a gap between the sheet of iron and the wall. We lay quiet again, listening for any suspicious sound. There was none.

The second board had to be prized up by lifting it with the iron plate. This was more difficult but with the two ends freed it came away. The iron plate was now proud and the next job was to slip it back to expose the third board. I got the crowbar underneath it and could not get it to move. I then got the bar further underneath it and Jock could stretch and pull the edge of the iron from his side. A big heave, the iron moved and then there was a sickening feeling of sudden loss of resistance followed by a thundering noise as the whole stove and chimney pipe crashed to the ground. It was a terrifying sound and the natural reaction was to scramble out of the hole as fast as possible. Standing in the room we both listened intently and there was no sound. I got back into the hole to get my mackintosh and other things while Jock went to look out of the window. It was almost dark but not quite.

'Look out,' said Jock, 'there is someone with a torch coming. Stay where you are.' Jock pushed the iron sheet back over the hole and put the stove upright. He did not have time to put the chimney piping back before the sound of boots came to the front door. The door of our room was wide open but prevented from going right back by the sofa Jock got over the sofa and hid behind the door. The sentry came down the corridor, opened the door of my bedroom, apparently had a look round and then came to our room. He stood at the door for a few ghastly seconds, shining his torch round the room and for some reason decided that the cause of the noise was not there. Perhaps he was as frightened as we were but miraculously after looking in two more rooms he decided to abandon his hunt and left the building.

Jock pushed the stove back to let me out and flopped on to the couch exhausted. I realised why when I crawled out and stood up. My legs were weak and shaky, it was like getting out of bed for the first time after a long illness. Carefully I peered out of the window. Snow was whistling around between the huts and in the distance was a torch bobbing up and down and shining at one door after another. The scene outside was bleak in the extreme and we were going to regret leaving this snug warm hole with parcels of food and a spirit stove. I flopped on to the sofa with Jock and we sat listening to the wind but there was no more sound of intruders.

It was bitterly cold and we decided to dress. Jock had a brown rolled neck pullover and a pair of dyed dark blue flannel trousers. The dye had taken unevenly and the appearance was blotchy. On top of this was a brown mack and on his head he put a blue beret. This, with his rather pointed nose and small moustache, gave an appearance that might be mistaken for a Frenchman, except perhaps by a Frenchman himself. His shoes were once black and badly worn. I wore some brown flannel trousers and a blue rolled neck sweater and an obvious British army mack and could not possibly have been mistaken for a Frenchman, but I had a good pair of shoes which were a great asset. Round our waists inside our shirts we stuffed the food, biscuits, cheese, bully beef, chocolate, cigarettes and matches and I put several lumps of sugar into my trouser pockets.

The boards, iron plates, stove and chimney piping were all put back and then a final inspection assured us that all was in order before departing. The first object was to locate the guard to find out if the front gate was manned. Quietly we tip-toed down the corridor, gingerly opened the front door and then emerged into a blizzard of blowing powder snow. There were about three or four inches on the ground. The freezing wind lashed through our clothing, chilling our flesh into inactivity. Slowly negotiating each corner we made our way down between the huts towards the front gate. There was a moon somewhere behind the dense blanket of cloud and snow so that it was not pitch dark, it was possible to distinguish objects fifty yards away.

Coming round the side of one hut, we got a view of the main gate so decided to get inside a nearer hut and watch activities from the window. Fortunately the doors were at the back and we were able to get in and edge towards the window and get a good view of the gate. It was closed and the guard stood to one side with a rifle slung over his shoulder. He was stamping with his feet and banging his hands together and pacing up and down across the gate to ward off the effects of the cold.

'I wonder how long he is going to stay there?'

'Perhaps he will do a tour of the camp.'

As far as we could see he was the only guard on duty, but there might well be one or more patrolling the fence, which encircling the camp was about a quarter of a mile in length.

We waited there, watching for two hours, and the sentry stayed by the gate. There seemed to be no other on duty, but almost certainly there would be one other or more asleep in the guard hut.

Time was getting on and we had to get out of the camp; there was no going back. It meant climbing the barbed wire barricade and we knew this would not be easy. It consisted of two vertical fences ten feet high set eight feet apart. In between the two fences was a barbed wire entanglement quite impossible to negotiate without proper wire cutters, light and plenty of time, and we had none of these. The possibility of having to climb the barricade had occurred to us previously and we had hidden a twelve foot plank underneath one of the huts close to the fence.

Throughout our planning we had set our minds on hiding in the camp until all the guards had gone but now reluctantly we had to turn to the alternative and this meant finding the plank and getting it across the top of the wire out of sight of any guard. We got there by a roundabout route between the huts and to our great relief found it under the hut where we expected, free from snow. Before getting it out we decided to do a little reconnaissance of the barricade. Jock went one way and I the other. There was no sign of any patrol.

We heaved out the plank and from that moment it was all go. It was only twenty yards or so to the barricade and very soon we had it across the top of both fences. I went up first, climbed the inner fence and tested the plank. It was insufficiently secure for walking and so I went across on my bottom with a leg each side. Reaching the other fence I stood up and jumped. Jock followed close behind.

Suddenly there we both were outside the cage free as the wind. It was a wonderful feeling. We gave each other a bear hug and sped the field to the nearest hedge.

CHAPTER FIVE

Lost in the Snow

We were away. Behind us were the barbed wire horror, the grim sentries, many days of planning and months and months of frustration. At top speed we ran across the rough ground which lay between the boundary of the camp and the road, as much out of excitement as self-preservation, but our ears were pricked for shouting or the whistle of a bullet. None came and each moment that passed without a shot increased our confidence. We climbed through a hedge and found ourselves on a main road bordered with small houses. There was not a sound or a light from any of them. Rapidly we walked up the road for half a mile and then broke out into some open country to the right. The fields were covered with snow, dry and crisp, and as the wind blew across the tops of the hillocks it whipped up clouds of white powder. The moon was bright between intervals of scurrying clouds and the trees, faintly silhouetted, were visible against the dark background of the distance.

We were really away now and the feeling of being free, unfettered, with a plan in mind was a sensation never to be forgotten. One had an overwhelming relish of space, a desire to run for miles in all directions at once and a heedless abandon so that whatever happened next was of no importance provided that that moment, so vivid and intensely alive, would last a little longer. Years of boredom and frustration, of obscurity and confusion had fallen away disclosing a world scintillating with action. Everything seemed right and purposeful. The snow, pure white, sparkled in the moonlight and the shadows vibrated in purple and blue. The trees stood in exact harmony with the scene, displaying their wintry tracery for no other purpose than to please. The wind blew because it was alive and the intense cold penetrated because it was stimulating. We ourselves were marvellous, France was a wonderful country and the world a magnificent place to be in.

We pushed on across the frozen fields, sometimes walking, sometimes running, our nostrils steaming in the biting air, which burnt our ears and froze our hair. That night at any time would have been beautiful, but to us just released, out in it, dependent on it and free with it, was something beyond the ordinary run of things; it would have brought warmth to a stone, generosity to the avaricious or rhapsody to the uninspired. Through the half light of the moon we ran to the ever receding horizon without thought for dircction but confident that our way was right. Enraptured, in silence, we went.

Space and freedom were in hand
Down the measures of the land.
To kiss the earth, to touch the sky,
To skim the trees, perchance to fly,
To sense the night and speed the way
Was all we asked until the day
Should bring us home
Eternally.

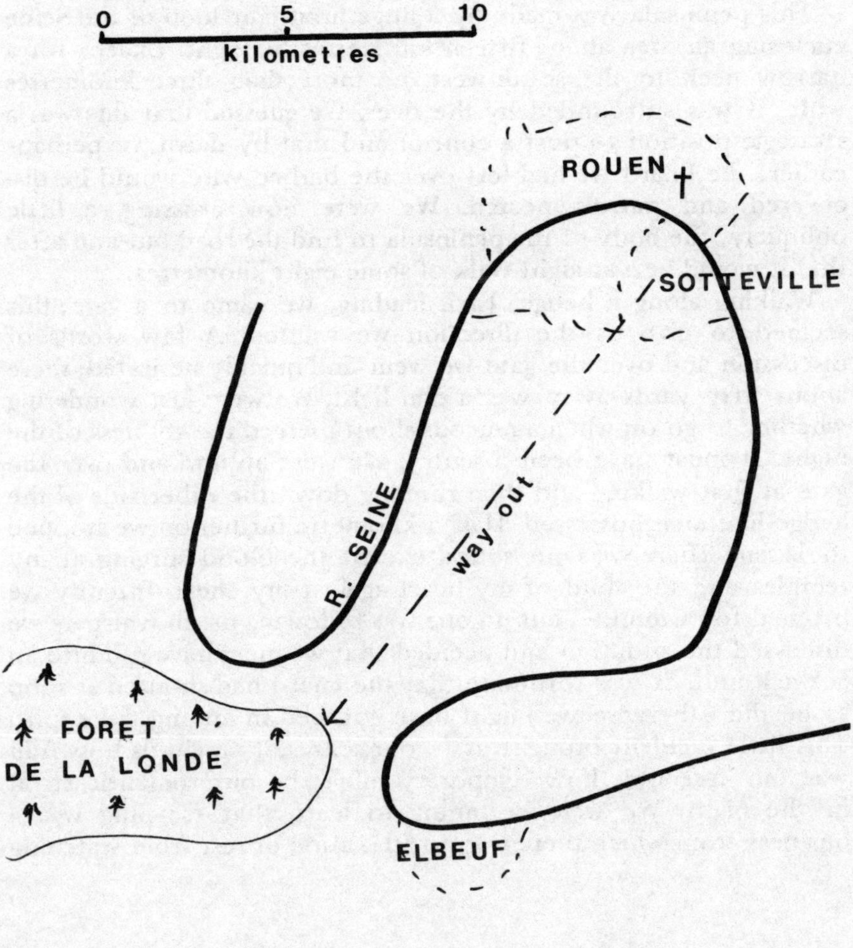

Gradually our pace settled down to a walk as our legs reminded us that they had been still for three days. It was now past midnight and we reckoned that there were nearly fifteen kilometres to cover before the dawn; on mid-European time this would mean about eight o'clock. Fifteen kilometres in eight hours seemed an easy task, but we had no compass and as the moon went down and the sky clouded over it was difficult to keep within several points of the right direction. Now and again we got a glimpse of the Pole Star which was a help. We had crossed the main road from Rouen to Elbeuf and were now making across country to the road along the western side of the peninsula leading through Grand Couronne to Moulineaux. Once there we should be through the narrow neck of the flask-shaped piece of land and could strike south into the forest.

This peninsula was made by a huge luxuriant loop of the Seine enclosing an area about fifteen kilometres by eight. Except for a narrow neck to the south-west, no more than three kilometres wide, it was surrounded by the river. We guessed that this was a strategic position to post a control and that by dawn, or perhaps earlier, the board we had left over the barbed wire would be discovered and patrols posted. We were now crossing, a little obliquely, the body of the peninsula to find the road out and after that it would be a straight walk of some eight kilometres.

Walking along a hedge, Jock leading, we came to a gate; this seemed to give us the direction we wanted. A few words of discussion and over the gate we went and quickly hesitated; there about fifty yards away was a dim light. We were just wondering whether to go on when a raucous shout pierced the stillness of the night. It must have been a sentry. We were around and over the gate at first walking and then running down the other side of the hedge like men possessed. Half a kilometre further on we stopped to listen. There was no sound except the blood surging at my temples and the thud of my heart against my chest. Intently we listened for a minute, but no one was following us. In whispers we discussed the situation and decided that we must have run into an ack-ack unit. It was fortunate that the guard had shouted as soon as he did otherwise we might have got well in amongst the unit. This little incident brought us to our senses, it taught us how frail was our freedom, how temporary might be our romantic stroll in the night. We were beginning to learn that escaping was a business from which there was no relaxation or rest from watching for the slightest sign of change in events.

Considerable time was wasted climbing over ditches and through hedges, in one direction and another, but eventually we came to the back of some houses and skirting them found the road.

Half an hour later we were well into open country again. It seemed that there was marshy ground on the right as a duck had broken the silence with its raucous note and a curlew swooped above with its soul searching cry. Tired, we lay down by the road side listening to the curlew far away to the right, out over the river and then again over our heads. A last cry came from the distance and the night was still once more. The silence pressed in upon us our ears alert for the slightest sound. The wind hissed a little in the long grass and some way ahead a dog barked. We lay back our heads on our hands against the snow covered bank of the road.

'Look out!'

I had dozed off.

Headlights were bearing down on us. We scrambled further away from the edge of the road and lay flat on our stomachs. The car sped past its lights illuminating the country around and we followed it as it climbed a long hill before it disappeared some distance away.

'Do you think it is getting light?'

'I was wondering that.'

'It seems to be blacker to the east than anywhere else and yet the sky seems to be lighter.'

'Look!' said Jock pointing to the east. 'There is an outline of a hill there.'

I could see it now, a ridge of land but impossible to say how far away.

'It's probably lighter behind that.'

'Time we pushed on.'

We had not been walking five minutes when another pair of headlights appeared. Again we dived into the bank by the side of the road and lay flat. This was a Wehrmacht car and possibly up to no good as far as we were concerned. Our step increased and by the time we reached the village of Grand Couronne dawn was breaking fast. Caution took us away from the road up into the hills on the left side, these were heavily wooded and gave us good cover.

There were sounds of activity from the farms below, clanging of milk buckets, a creaking barn door, a sharp order to an animal and in the distance a boat hooted on the Seine.

We climbed steeply on to the top of the ridge and then picked our way along and so passed through the bottle neck into the edge of the Fôret de la Londe, our first objective.

We hoped to stay in the forest most of the day but had no accurate idea how large it was. The map which had been torn from a children's geography book was small scale, five kilometres to the centimetre. It gave no indication of the extent of the forest. It marked small country towns, not villages, the main roads and rivers. The point of destination lay roughly south-west from our present location and about forty kilometres as the crow flies.

There was only sparse undergrowth so that although we kept away from the paths walking was quite easy and the progress we made was rather too rapid. By midday we were on the further edge of the forest. Here we ran into a throng of youths dressed in the familiar grey, possibly men from a German forestry camp. They were busy felling trees and piling wood and appeared to take no notice of us as we passed through them. A sudden shout from one of the men in charge might have led us into suspicion had either of us turned round. The temptation to do so was great. We aped the imperviousness of the French peasant and listened for the second shout to come, taking care not to increase our step in the meantime. There was no second shout and no sound of anyone running after us. Round a turn in the path we breathed again. The trees thinned out giving way to pasture land. The path led on to a small road and here we had to decide whether to turn right or left. Left it was, possibly a wrong decision as it led quite away from the direction that we sensed but it kept us off a main road where we might easily have been picked up. The road ran along the south edge of the forest. For the next five kilometres we passed groups of youths from the forestry camp singing the usual Nazi songs which quite spoilt our walk along a pleasant country road.

Soon we came to a village and here there were gentle reminders of the pleasant things of life and my stomach got the better of caution.

'How about a drink?'

Jock looked a little surprised but not for long. A hopeful grin came to his face in affirmation. He had never been the sort to refuse that kind of invitation.

'I can't resist that.'

We selected a cottage which had a café sign over its door together with many other advertisements in varying stages of decay and disintegration. The door was closed but within a few seconds of our rapping it was opened by an old lady who wasted no time in looking us up and down. Drawing her conclusion, her impression was apparently unfavourable towards us because she made to shut the door but we were hot on the scent with thirst uppermost in our minds.

Jock held open the door and did a little pleading in the best French he could muster. He told her how we had been walking all day and were very thirsty and that all we needed was one drink and we should be on our way again. The old lady hesitated, Jock turned on his most charming smile and won the situation, hovering as we were on the very threshold of defeat. She opened the door wider and beckoned us in. The door led straightway into a front room. Here seated by a log fire in a little grate high from the floor was an old man and a girl perhaps ten or eleven years of age.

We sat down on a wooden bench by the window. The old man appeared not to have noticed us, continuing to look at the fire. The young girl had watched us come in but was either not interested or had a better reason for giving us no acknowledgement. She got up and left the room. We sat, our hands in our laps, awaiting events.

The old man quickly stole a glance at us and then returned to his fire-watching and an occasional suck on a clay pipe with a broken off stem.

'What do you want?' Madame had spoken abruptly as she poked her head round the door.

'Some wine, if you please.'

She looked grudgingly in our direction and withdrew. It was plain that no conversation was forthcoming from the old man so we sat in a silence that became more oppressive as each moment passed.

'It is very cold outside,' said Jock, but for all the response it brought from our host it might never have been said.

Five minutes passed very slowly. The door opened and in came Madame with two large glasses of steaming red wine. She placed them on the table in front of us, the little girl came in behind her and they both sat down on the other side of our table.

'This is magnificent,' I said, 'I did not know that one drank hot red wine. I have never seen it before.'

'In the winter,' said our hostess, and then conversation lapsed again.

With calculated accuracy the old man spat into the fire, a sizzle proclaimed that he found his target and he replaced the stump of the clay stem back into his mouth.

'Is it far from here to Elbeuf?'

'*Non*,' said the woman.

'About how far?'

She looked round at the old man but got no response. It is likely that she was as bad at judging distances as others of her sex. The little girl raised four fingers on her right hand and nodded her head nervously but this brought her an angry look from the gentleman with the pipe.

The wine was very hot and refreshing but the atmosphere in the room remained frigid and as the three sat there with glum expressions on their faces it became quite obvious that they wanted nothing but our departure. Something had to be done about this situation.

I raised my glass, looked at the old man and then at the woman. '*Vive la France*!'

This was followed with as friendly a smile as could be mustered. The effect was quite startling. The woman looked straight at us and in a deep whisper said, '*Oui, la France*.'

'*La belle France*,' added Jock.

The old man drew his chair to the table and raised his pipe to us.

'You have come a long way?'

'Yes, a long way.'

'Are you working in the Forest?'

'No, we are making for Neubourg, to work on a farm there.'

'Yes – you must be tired.'

'My granddaughter,' he added with pride, as he turned to the girl and touched her under the chin.

'You are very lucky.'

'Yes, sometimes I am, but she teases her grandfather a lot, don't you, my pretty?'

Meanwhile Madame had disappeared. Now she returned with two more glasses of wine.

'You must be cold and thirsty! I thought you had come from the camp in the Forest. There are many people working there for the Germans.'

At that moment the temptation, magnified by the effect of the wine, to open up was considerable but a glance from Jock had a sobering effect and the urge to increase our friendship passed. We were on route with a definite plan and this was no time or place to get involved.

'No, we are on our way to Neubourg to work on a farm.'

'You have a long way to go. How far is it Grandpapa?'

'Oh, about twenty-five kilometres, if you walk hard you will get there this evening. I have never done it on my own feet, only on a horse.'

'Grandpapa never walks any further than the end of the garden' – she smiled – 'and then only when it is necessary.'

Grandpapa looked a little hurt.

'What do you think of my Marie?'

'A lovely girl, is she as good as she looks?'

'Never, she needs her father here.'

Marie looked sad and dropped her head. A few seconds later she looked up and said slowly.

'My father is a prisoner of war in Germany.'

'She has not seen him for over two years,' added her grandmother. Here again the temptation to confide in them was great, but we suppressed it and fell into silence.

They looked at us from over the table, perhaps sensing our predicament.

'Some more wine?'

'No we must get on our way, thank you, if we are to get to Neubourg tonight. Another glass and I shall be asleep by the side of the road.'

We rose and made to go.

Madame went to the window and parted the curtains a little. 'Wait a minute,' she said sharply. Three youths in grey uniform were passing and as we waited and listened their boots resounded on the cobblestones outside.

Madame muttered something low and rasping between her teeth and a sizzle from the fire indicated once more that Grandad had found his target. Marie stood on one leg and bit the end of her long plait of hair.

The noise of their boots faded away and Madame opened the door. Shaking hands, we thanked her, and passing through the door she pressed a little packet of biscuits into our palms. Soon we were away down the street feeling refreshed and sensing that we were in a friendly country.

We were heading for Elbeuf, which we knew was a place to avoid. Elbeuf would be a key point for a control, so we turned south down the first small road, a route unmarked on our map.

For three hours the going was easy and we had got well into the country away from any main roads. As the effect of the wine wore off, the cold of evening and fatigue soon started to slow our pace. We sat down by the roadside and opened our packet of biscuits.

'How about turning in for a bit and then walking for the rest of the night? I feel pretty tired,' I said.

'It will be hard to find our way at night without stars, and it doesn't look very helpful at present,' added Jock.

'It's safer walking at night, we can see car lights approaching and be in the ditch before they are on to us.'

'I am all for a rest now, these shoes are the devil.'

We pulled ourselves on to our feet and started walking again looking out for somewhere to lie down. During the next kilometre or so there was no suitable haystack or barn and we decided to make for a wood, a field away from the road.

Two pairs of sticks stuck into the ground and tied together at the top with a cross bar made the starting of a framework for a shelter and to this we lashed other sticks crosswise with bracken stalks. Dead bracken lay thick on the ground. We gathered it in armfuls putting a thick layer on the floor to act as a mattress and then bound large bunches of it to fill in the roof and sides. A large pile closed in the foot and another at the other end was to pull over our bodies and our heads after getting into position. By the time we had finished it was dark. We lit a little fire, pulled out the bully tin and made our second hot drink that day from melted snow.

A little light, a little warmth and all around was cold and dark. A steady biting breeze filtered through the trees and penetrated our not very numerous garments but in spite of that a sense of incomparable peace and tranquillity settled upon me as I lay on my side supported on one elbow looking at the fire. Jock was gazing into the fire too, he had taken his shoes off and rested his stockinged feet on the outside of the uppers. Now and again he wriggled his toes as if to restore the circulation. The fire died down and both of us were too lazy and too frozen into inactivity to get up and fetch more wood.

'What's the time?'

'Quarter past seven.'

'It's time we turned in.'

'Give me two of those sleeping tablets.'

Jock put his shoes on, stamped out the fire and added a few handfuls of snow to put the finishing touch to what embers remained.

We took two tablets each and then prepared to turn in. One of our macks laid over the bracken was used as a ground sheet and the other to cover us over. It took a lot of manoeuvring to get into position in a very confined space and complete the covering up process.

We curled up together like the babes in the wood, embarrassment gradually conceding to the cold as we pressed closer and closer to make a snug fit. We lay thus for two hours or more neither daring to move lest he disturb the other and both feigning sleep with closed eyes and breathing gently. The bracken rustled close to our heads, little pieces dropping on to our cheeks, causing a degree of irritation only experienced when one's hands are unavailable. Spiders and other hurrying insects moved about just close to our ears. Eventually the cold became so penetrating that we were forced to admit to each other that we were both wide awake. It was a discouraging outlook, ten hours of darkness with nothing to relieve the monotony of continuous walking. We scrambled out of our little hut and brushed the bracken off. There had been a lot more snow, the trees were laden and the boundaries of the road almost obliterated by the drifts which had piled up on either side of the hedgerows. The wind blew in icy gusts, anchoring our clothing to our bodies and penetrating it with the ease of summer wear. It whipped the snow in whirling clouds of powder, passing over the hedge tops and pouring through the narrow gaps in hissing, stinging streams. Somewhere behind this deluge of the elements the firmament provided a moon but it was of not much help on this journey. Conditions were desolate suggestive of northern Siberia or Alaska. In some places the road was bordered by ditches, quite untraceable and into which we stumbled quite often to our knees or to the top of our thighs or waists. We plodded on through the night, from one drift to another, making slow progress, talking very little, isolated by the elements and occupied by the physical difficulties of walking.

A signpost protruded from the top of a drift. The meagre light from the moon was insufficient to read it by. Jock gave me a bunk up the centre post, and spreading my mackintosh over the directing arm, struck a match beneath it and had a fleeting glance before it blew out. The names were none that we remembered from our map. They must have been villages which were little help to us.

For eight hours we trudged along country roads first in one direction and then in another. No road continued for long in the direction that our instinct or sense of locality prompted us. The signposts were no help, for we never saw a name given by the map. At the end of that time we were practically all in. Jock did not complain of his feet but by the way he was walking I knew that they were giving him considerable trouble.

A shed appeared out of the darkness on the left hand side of the road. We felt for the door, pushed the snow away and barged it open. Seldom could a shed full of hay have brought greater joy, the relief of pushing the door shut, away from the wind and the driving snow, the calm, the still dense darkness, the confined security. Here was peace, tranquillity, the cessation of the weather and relaxation from the constant lifting of one foot in front of the other.

We scrambled to the top of the stack and burrowed our way well beneath the surface. A frightened rat scampered to the wall, the stalks cracked in our ears and warmth came upon us as we fell asleep.

As I regained consciousness and tried to think where I was, the horror of the walk through the night and the relief of crawling into this place flashed back. Daylight was showing through the cracks and the wind seemed to have died down because it was possible to hear regular breathing from Jock's quarter suggesting that he was still asleep. I lay there revelling in the blessing of warmth and going over the plan for the day. We must now be at least thirty-five kilometres from Rouen in an area that they would never think of searching unless someone had been suspicious and reported us. It would obviously be thought, especially in this weather, that the most obvious hiding place would be Rouen or some other town. It was important to get to Beaumont-le-Roger today so as to hide up and get out of sight but getting there meant walking on the roads, cross-country was impossible. This was a risk that had got to be taken. We had no idea how far it was but a guess of somewhere between fifteen and twenty-five kilometres was in my mind and we should, on roads, be able to make five kilometres an hour. Beaumont-le-Roger we imagined was a small country town and Anthony de Salis whom I had known in Elbersdorf had told us that his relations lived in the château. This was the object of the first stage of our journey. For no other reason had we thrust out in this direction and as time passed we optimistically built up greater and greater hopes of what was to be gained. We thought of food and hiding and possibly some advice on how to get out of France because Anthony came from a cosmopolitan, diplomatic family with international connections and it was reasonable to expect some help from this quarter.

'Jock.' I nudged him and he groaned a bit and then lay in silence.

'How do you feel?' There was still no immediate reply.

'Not brilliant but I'm all right.'

'Do you feel like going?'

'Oh yes, just give me a few moments.'

It was worrying, Jock was not his usual jovial self and was obviously not feeling up to scratch, but if we could just get to Beaumont-le-Roger he could rest up and get over whatever it was. His feet were giving him a lot of trouble. He had come away with the best pair of shoes he could get but they were too large and an attempt to pad the toes with paper had caused chafing and his heels were blistered.

By 8.30 a.m. we were under way, having had a couple of hours' good sleep. Jock did not look well and I knew he must be feeling lousy to be so quiet, but we kept going, which was important, on a road which by our reckoning was running almost due south. The sun was not out but we caught hazy glimpses of it amongst dense clouds, enough to get some idea of direction.

In front of us came into view a milk urn, standing on a small platform apparently awaiting collection. Could it be full? It was and the idea of its contents suddenly made us realize how hungry and thirsty we were. It had a tap near the top and on tipping out came the cream of the can. We took turns to open our mouths like young cuckoos and drank to the full. If ever there was nectar that was it, still warm from the morning's milking. After an hour's walk we came to a village and to our joy there was a road junction with a sign to Neubourg; it was seven kilometres. Beaumont was another ten kilometres so we had, all going well, about three and a half hours' walk. Things looked better and we decided to turn into a café. We flopped into two chairs away from the muster of men round the bar. Everyone was drinking hot red wine, and fortunately Madame assumed that we would do likewise and brought two glasses to us, eliminating the necessity of our exposing our accent in front of a lot of locals.

'*Voilà, Messieurs*.'

We nodded our gratitude mumbling *merci* and were perfectly content to sit and sip the mulled brew in silence. It was fortunate that we had plenty of French money. In the camp at Sotteville we had all been paid in French currency unlike the camps in Germany where a special *lager gelt* was used. In Sotteville money could only be used for buying what was available in the camp shop, which was nothing more than toilet articles and stationery, there was no refreshment of any kind. The main purpose of money was for gambling. Bridge and poker passed the time for most of the inmates every evening and sometimes all day and it was common knowledge who the rich men were. Jock and I had borrowed plenty with no more security than a promise to repay after the war and it was a wonderful reserve to have. A canvas bag containing money, prisoner of war disc, crucifix and British officer's identity card hung from my neck. We had yet to learn exactly what could be bought without ration cards; drinks and shellfish were available we knew because these had often secretly been bought through the German guard and it was nothing unusual to have champagne and oysters in exchange for a considerable amount of French currency or to their preference British chocolate or cigarettes.

The gentlemen at the bar filtered out and we asked for some more wine. Jock told me that he was feeling ill and that he thought the best plan was for me to push on and get to Beaumont-le-Roger and find out what was happening at the château. He felt too ill to walk another twelve miles. He would find a haystack and lie up until tomorrow and he pointed out that this plan had the advantage of a single strange person on the open road being less conspicuous than two. Tomorrow he would get there and meet me in the church nearest the château at four in the afternoon. In the event of my drawing a blank at the château the only possible plan was to return here, make contact, and go back to Rouen where we knew of an address. Then we discussed how to make contact and this café seemed to be the obvious place. We estimated that I could be back here by midday so Jock said that he would be in this café by 11.30 a.m. and wait until midday and if there was no sign of me proceed to Beaumont-le-Roger so as to keep his rendezvous in the church by 4 p.m.

'Where are you going to lie up?'

'Oh, I will find a place, if not I shall go back to the hay shed. It's far better for you to get on and find out what's happening at the château. If that is no help, the sooner we know the better.'

It was a bad plan, hurriedly conceived, but seeming adequate at the time. Outside the café Jock said, 'Be seeing you – all the best.'

'Cheerio – until tomorrow.'

That was the last we ever saw of each other.

By ten o'clock I had got through Neubourg and was on a straight road running south-west to Beaumont. It was a fine day, freezing hard, but the sun was out and there was a light wind. I walked fast and in the more concealed parts broke into a jog so that progress was good and I met no one and was only passed by one truck. The road was absolutely straight, climbing up a gradual slope to what I assumed was the edge of a river valley before going downhill into the town.

Looking up to the crown of the hill, some three kilometres away, I could see a black object by the side of the road. It looked remarkably like a control hut and as I got nearer I could distinguish a sentry walking up and down outside it. This was a severe blow and needed some quick thinking. I dare not risk trying to pass this point without papers but continued walking looking for the next turning off. There was no way back apart from abandoning the whole plan of getting to Beaumont. The only hope was a partial detour so as to enter the town by another route, but it was wishful thinking to hope that other routes were not controlled. The hut indicated that the control was not just a temporary affair set up for us but something associated with the area or town.

I found a lane leading to the left and walked for some distance. At first it was very exposed but later passed through woods where it was little more than a cart track covered with undisturbed snow. A lane leading off to the right in the direction of the town attracted me because it might lead down the hill into the outskirts of the town without attracting sufficient importance for a control. On the left side was some open country with a large farm house and a group of farm buildings but further on the lane passed through more wooded land.

I plodded on, meeting no one and a quarter of an hour later came to another stretch of open land extending over the brow of the hill. To my horror there was a runway on the right and about half a dozen planes standing out in the open, on the left the woods continued and I could see hangars hidden among the trees. The track had a small barbed wire fence each side and seemed to lead on straight through the aerodrome.

While I continued to walk the decision to turn back was uppermost in my mind but a few moments later, mounting the top of the hill, I could see some men walking from the runway in the direction of this track. It was too late, I had to go on and run the gauntlet and as our paths converged I could see that these men were in civilian working clothes and looked like French labourers. They walked apart, without conversation, toward a break in the fence some hundred yards or so ahead and by gradually quickening my pace I was able surreptitiously to join the rear of the party. It was difficult to believe my luck especially when other groups emerged and joined us as we went along. Further on the barbed wire fence became higher and there was a larger gate on both sides each manned by a sentry but by then I felt fully secure sticking to the group, looking glum, walking alone and saying nothing. By the time we got to the main gate and sentry box there was a general exodus of workers going out for lunch and the sentry was not interested in anyone going out but I saw him examine the pass of a civilian going in.

The main gate opened out on to a busy road, it was from Neubourg, the one which I had left on the other side of the hill. It ran downhill into the town, curved with high wooded banks on each side and these were crowded with huts. The Frenchmen dispersed, some of them going down into the town where the way became more and more busy with groups of Luftwaffe coming and going in and out of the various huts.

The picturesque country town nestled under the escarpment of the plateau, which bestrode a little river with attractive old bridges and banks adorned with icy layers. The streets were crowded with men in uniform, groups hanging round cafés and shops and some, like servicemen the world over, busy searching for presents for wives and girlfriends.

So elated and pleased was I at successfully bypassing the control and getting into the place that little thought had been given to the next move. The original plan, when we imagined that Beaumont-le-Roger was a quiet little country town, was simply to call at the château and introduce oneself but caution got the better of me. I was not at all confident that the château was a good place to go until I had found out more about it. There was nothing that I had seen to persuade me that Beaumont was anything but a highly dangerous place in which to hesitate or linger or to knock on strange doors. What was wanted was a little advice from an old inhabitant who knew what was happening at the château and whether the family was still in residence.

Without further thought I found myself going towards the church. It was a lovely imposing building half way up the hill on the north side. Entering through the west door I heard singing and carefully selected an inconspicuous pew well to the back. There were some twenty or thirty schoolgirls engaged in choir practice and taking them was an old curé with white hair and a very red face. No one took any notice of my entry and it was a great relief to get off the streets, to sit unnoticed in a dark corner and have time to think. I watched the curé, he was entirely absorbed by his pupils and they it seemed by him. He had a little stick and walked around gently tapping the tops of the choir stalls looking at one girl after another in a benign objective way.

I sat there lulled by the voices and the music and the peace and tranquillity of the church, knowing without doubt that here was the person of choice for information about the family in the château. The blood began to circulate in my limbs and I passed into a state of semi-consciousness and remained so until alerted by the chatter and patter of many feet coming down the aisle. There was a pause in the chatter as they spotted me sitting under a large column and I purposely avoided the glances of the little angels as they passed. The curé was busy collecting the music from the stalls and when they had gone I knew the time had come to take the plunge. He must have seen me before because as I approached he registered no surprise but stood there with a receptive expression and waited for me to open the conversation.

In halting French I asked him if he could spare a moment to give me some advice. Without hesitation he turned round and led the way to a little room at the east end. Here I told him that I was a British officer escaped from a German camp in Rouen and immediately plunged my hand inside my shirt to get out the celluloid container which hung round my neck. I showed him my British identification card and my prisoner of war disc. He asked me what he could do to help and I told him that I wanted to know who was living in the château because one of the relations of the family who was in the camp at Rouen had advised me to go there. He registered some alarm by raising both arms and told me that it was an officers' mess and that the owners had gone to live in Paris. He went on to explain that the Luftwaffe had recently come here to establish a night fighter aerodrome and that there were Germans in almost every house. He himself was left with only one room to live in. Had this unit not been here he would gladly have taken me in for the night but it was quite impossible and he advised me to get out of the town as soon as possible. I thanked him deeply for his help and hoped that my contact with him had brought him no danger.

As I left the Church my heart sank very low. Here was our plan completely shattered; poor as it may have been we had optimistically built up great hope and faith in it as a rallying point and a possible solution of getting out of France. I had pictured myself that very night with my knees under the table of a French family with the prospects of a comfortable bed and some change of clothing.

Such was my depression that there was a strong desire to throw caution to the wind and ask for a room in one of the hotels but I compromised and went into a café for a drink. I asked for a beer and took it to a corner and sat there watching the Luftwaffe playing a table form of skittles by swinging a ball on a string. It was then about 4 p.m. and I knew that I had to get out of the town. It was no good going back the same way past the aerodrome, the same luck could not possibly happen twice. What the curé had said explained very well the odd circumstances which had let me enter the town. I had obviously come in the back of the aerodrome which was under construction and the fences were not yet finished. I decided to go out by the road going north and then veer round across country in the dark so as to join up again with the road back to Neubourg. Getting out into the town again with the streets swarming with Luftwaffe, a sudden hatred of the place overwhelmed me and became so intense that I almost broke into a run to get out as quickly as possible but I managed to stem the urge and walked, selecting a road marked Brionne and Pont-Audemer, by the river which I knew would lead me north. As it got dark I cut across country in the hope of coming out on to the road to Neubourg, once there I should feel safe about keeping the rendezvous with Jock by 11.30 the next morning. It would be fatal to miss contact and to let him go on into the Beaumont trap.

Two hours later I broke out on to the road which was a relief and little further on came to a farm by the roadside. Walking into the yard I saw a wagon loaded with straw and suddenly everything in me seemed to yearn for that haven. I climbed up on to the top and made a big trench into which I crept and covered myself over, shivering and shaking in the anticipation of warmth. In my shirt were still a packet of biscuits and two portions of wrapped-up cheese and in my trouser pockets about six lumps of sugar. Two biscuits, one piece of cheese and two lumps of sugar were eaten slowly and meticulously, making the most of every morsel.

Sleep came soon after and I knew nothing more until I was suddenly awake with banging and shouting of no mean fury going on at my feet. Sheepishly and very frightened I crawled out and stood up at the side of the wagon and there was a little man waving a pitchfork. When he saw me he shouted loud and angrily and the more I tried to get a word in the more he increased his noise. It reminded me of the defensive bark of a dog which fears to stop lest it lose mastery of the situation. The closer one approaches the louder and more vicious it gets.

I jumped down and seized the man's hand and said, '*Je suis votre ami, monsieur.*' He immediately became quiet and looked me very thoroughly up and down.

'*Qui êtes vous*?' he asked and I replied, '*Un prisonnier de guerre s'échappé d'Allemagne*' and carefully avoided saying from Rouen.

'*Vous êtes anglais*?'

'*Oui.*'

He was now quite friendly and told me he had thought that I was a deserter from the German army, but he probably only said that for my benefit. He had probably been walking round his farm last thing at night and noticed a pair of boots sticking out from the straw. My feet are anything but dainty and he must have been alarmed by the sight. He took me to his best barn, got me some sacks and with his hands scooped out a nice berth in the chaff. Then he disappeared and by the time the barn door creaked open again I was well covered with sacks and chaff. To my unbelievable joy he carried in his hand a plate with a large piece of bread and some cheese. He stood at my feet talking and talking watching with glee the pleasure that his refreshment had brought. For half an hour he continued in a brogue that I found very difficult to understand until finally noticing my increasing unresponsiveness he approached, shook me warmly by the hand and mumbled '*Bonne chance.*' It was a touching moment to herald a safe night's sleep.

When I woke grey light was coming through the ill-fitting barn doors. Pushing aside the chaff and removing the sacks I rose and spent some time getting rid of the chaff. It meant stripping completely and shaking all my clothes, it really was a devil of a job and at the end I was by no means free of it. With my shoes and mackintosh on I set off quietly leaving the barn and the yard without attempting to make any contact in case anyone else was around who might bring danger to either party. I was on the road by 7.30 a.m. which gave me just four hours to keep the rendezvous with Jock. It was about seven kilometres to Neubourg and the same distance beyond which at five kilometres per hour gave me some time to spare.

After an uneventful journey I got to the café in good time hoping to find Jock already there but he was not. I ordered a hot red wine and got cosily snuggled in a corner by the fire. There was no one else in the café. I sat there thinking and hoping, looking out of the window, gazing at the fire, snatching a glance at my watch and wondering what to do if Jock did not appear.

11.30 a.m. passed and there was no Jock. I waited until 11.50 a.m. and then decided to ask Madame before anyone else appeared.

'*Vous avez vu quelque chose de mon ami, Madame*?'

'*Mais non, Monsieur.*'

'*Nous étions un rendezvous ici à onze heures et demi.*'

'*Ou, la, la – comment faire*?'

'*Je ne sais pas, j'attendrai un peu.*'

'*Encore du vin*?'

'*S'il vous plait.*'

During the remaining twenty minutes there my mind was working fast. Maybe Jock was too ill to get here, maybe he had been captured or maybe he had gone on prematurely but in the latter event he would surely have come to the café first and left a message with Madame.

Had he already gone on we would surely have met on the road, unless he had decided to go the night before. The idea of going all the way to Beaumont to keep the date in the church with him at 4 p.m. was repugnant to me, it meant going back by a detour round to the north side of the town and it would be impossible to get there before 7 p.m., three hours late.

I decided to walk back to our shed of hay where we had spent two hours during the first night; it was the only place that I knew where he might be.

An hour later I searched the place but there was no evidence in the shed that he had been there or any fresh foot marks in the snow outside.

I decided to return to the café once more and on my way there evolved a plan if there was no sign of him. I would go to the church and try and find the curé and ask if he had heard anything.

There was still no sign of Jock at the café and I made my way to the church. It was empty. I found the curé in his house. Not unnaturally he was hesitant about letting me in but on my asking for a word with him he beckoned me into the hall and closed the front door.

'Is it possible to telephone M. le Curé at Beaumont-le-Roger, because I was meeting someone in the church there at 4 p.m. and wanted to ask him to tell the person that I was unable to keep the appointment?' If I could have a word with the curé there he would remember me and give the same advice to Jock.

The curé looked at me.

'*Vous êtes anglais?*'

'*Oui.*'

'*Je crois votre ami est pris par les gendarmes. J'ai entendu, il y a une demi-heure depuis.*'

There was a horrible silence and I realised very acutely that I was not a welcome visitor.

I later learned that Jock had been discovered in a haystack and handed over to the Germans. He returned to POW life in Germany.

I left quickly and wandered down the road opposite to the way I had approached. It was urgent that I get out of the district as quickly as possible. Keeping to the road was dangerous but walking across open farm land in broad daylight was even more obvious. There was nothing to do but trudge on and hope that the news of Jock's capture and his identity would be slower in dispersal than my walking pace.

In the café I had studied the map with the idea of returning to Rouen by train. The nearest point with a railway station was Brionne and this was somewhere between sixteen and twenty kilometres from the café. The decision to make for this very soon became a fix.

During that afternoon's walk the awful realisation of Jock's capture came over me with a cloak of depression heavy enough to make my feet drag. Jock had gone, our plan was wrecked, my food had nearly gone, I was dog-tired and the village behind me was now possibly buzzing with the talk of a roaming Englishman. If Jock had been caught in the district how was it that I had come in afterwards and not been taken?

While in the camp we had been given an address in Rouen, but had been advised not to go there unless other plans failed because it had been used for some time and had probably either closed or been changed. I had it firmly fixed in my memory and it now seemed the only thing left to go for. The idea of walking back to Rouen alone was impracticable and the sooner I got off these roads the better. A train would get me across the Seine and avoid crossing one of the bridges by foot where a control would be likely.

Eventually I got to the centre of Brionne and noticed a small suitable hotel and my bones told me that that was to be my home for the night. I had had my fill of hay, chaff, straw and bracken. Whatever the risk it would be worth it. The town was comparatively free of Germans. There was one vehicle with a driver standing outside a building labelled *Stadt Kommandatur*.

I entered the hotel and sat down at a table inside the door. Madame came up to me and asked me what I would take, the answer was now obvious: *'Un vin chaud, s'il vous plait.' 'Oui, Monsieur.'* When she returned I asked her if it was possible to have a room for the night. Without hesitation she said yes and asked me what time I would like dinner. The temptation was almost overwhelming and I came very near to telling her who I was and asking for dinner without ration cards but at the last moment caution won and I explained to her that I was very tired and would go to bed as soon as possible. She seemed surprised that anyone should want to go to bed at seven in the evening but within fifteen minutes my room was ready and it was all mine, a lovely bed and twelve hours for sleep.

As I undressed chaff fell in a ring round my feet. I washed all over from the bidet and dried as well as possible with a handkerchief and then slid into bed under a welcoming duvet.

In the morning a small jug of water was pushed through the door. I lay still awhile feeling a different person, rested and at peace, confident that any increased risk of coming here had been amply justified. Having dressed and taken great care to clear up all the chaff piece by piece and washed it down in the bidet I went downstairs and sat in the hall. Madame greeted me with a reassuring smile but my face fell when she produced a long white form and indicated that it should be filled in, apologising for not having presented it on the previous evening. I knew exactly what it was and had in fact expected it but by now was wishfully hoping that it would elude me.

The usual questions were asked, name, place of birth, occupation, home address, reason for travelling, duration of stay, number and type of identification papers. A student receiving an examination paper for which he was completely unprepared would have sympathised with me at that moment. I sat down and with as much imagination as possible attempted to create an episode in the life of a travelling Frenchman.

He turned out to be Paul Marin, a bank clerk visiting his sick mother in Rouen. It was the birth date which had me on the brink. I wrote June and then quickly scratched it out for Juin. I made up a figure for the identification papers. Madame had been standing just behind me and when the paper was handed over she studied it carefully, said, '*Bien*' and then went to her desk and produced the bill which was paid without any difficulty.

I smiled at Madame, thanked her for her warm welcome and bade her adieu. '*Au revoir, Monsieur*', she said with a smile, which reassured me that she would not need to ask any more questions.

I left the hotel with elation and a feeling of gratitude to my friendly, lenient and intelligent examiner. On many occasions it was obvious that a French person is very quick at individual assessment, I was to meet another within a quarter of an hour.

At the station there was a queue for the ticket office and when it came to my turn I said quite simply:

'*Rouen, s'il vous plait*.'

'*Comment*?'

For a Britisher the pronunciation of this name is difficult.

I repeated it twice and still the man at the other side of the hole did not register and started to look suspicious. Things were clicking fast and he must have been on the verge of asking for my papers as was frequently their habit, when from over my shoulder, in a very authoritative manner came a female voice:

'*Rrrouen*.'

The ticket was there without more ado and as I turned to go my eyes caught those of a smartly dressed middle-aged lady. She had a slight smile and a kindly awareness in her bright eyes. She gave the impression of an expert diagnostician and it recharged my failing confidence.

CHAPTER SIX

The Haven of Rouen

The train pulled into Rouen Station about midday. Long before reaching its destination the occupants of the compartment had begun to make ready. Their conversation, which had been abundant during the whole journey, ceased. The carrier racks, overladen to breaking point, contained every imaginable type of package. Bundles rested on their knees and the space under the seat was stuffed to capacity. There could be no doubt that the struggle was going to be desperate if all these people with all their packages were going to have the precedence of exit that each imagined. They loaded their burdens with precision and a finality resulting from ample practice. Like soldiers refreshed from a halt on a march they manoeuvred and wriggled the upper part of their anatomy into the various straps and strings which distributed the weight of their luggage.

When this was done they turned towards the estimated door of arrival and braced themselves for the plunge. The drill was not carried out without a trace of delicacy and politeness typical of the natives of this country on such an occasion. There were apologies as they pushed and trod on each other's toes and worked like ones possessed in this desperate struggle for survival. But at this moment of departure the inherited element of courtesy became eclipsed by a zest, born of the condition of war, to serve the demands of the omnipotent black market. A little more 'push' was justifiable; a little more heightening of the colour and dilation of the veins of the forehead revealed the urgency of the situation.

As soon as the platform came in sight the handles were turned to the ready and the doors allowed to remain ajar. Now there was deathly silence as every face leaned towards the exit. Mouths were tightly closed and limbs were braced for the spring. It came. What a mad rush it was; with what incredible speed twenty people with twice, nay thrice, as many packages, could escape through a small door. This miracle of birth could never have happened without some element of grace and concession.

For me there was no hurry. I remained seated watching this astounding performance from within. It was as well, however, to keep within the crowd so as not to be one of the stragglers through the barrier. Fortunately I had chosen the middle of the train.

What a picture of movement as everyone raced to the barrier, a fusion of individuality bent upon one object, a scene of distortion as the weight of their burdens played havoc with their legs. What a medley of boots and clogs and shoes and slippers, of berets, shawls and kepis, of short jackets and long coats trailing on the ground, of blue trousers, leggings, knee breeches, aprons and skirts. Like schoolboy athletes in a walking race some allowed themselves to break into the semblance of a run but most kept to the rules and walked as fast as their legs would move.

As I approached the barrier in apprehension, gripping my ticket in a hot wet palm, my eyes were alert for a control but there was no trouble. At other barriers there were military police and queues for departure platforms were having their cards examined by gendarmes. This control, I learned later, was for all passengers leaving the station and was looking for us because it was thought that we were still in Rouen and would sooner or later make an attempt to leave.

Out of the station there was a great sense of relief and increased security among the crowds on the streets and one felt much less conspicuous.

In the centre of the town there were many in German uniform, some smart and others not so smart but mostly with an air of detachment making a point it seemed, quite contrary to their usual behaviour, of not pushing other pedestrians off the pavement. Rouen was a leave centre for the district and at this particular stage of the war when Germany was still in the ascendancy planning to build the new Europe, orders had gone around that civilians of the occupied territories were to be treated with a degree of respect. They walked about mainly in twos gazing into the shops.

The possibility of being recognised by one of the guards or staff from the camp suddenly occurred to me but on reflection I decided that the Commandant and doctor had now almost certainly left the district and that the guard or supply staff would be unlikely to recognise me even if they saw me close to, but the idea brought a sense of self-consciousness. I felt in a ragged state and my mackintosh was torn at the back and was recognisable as a British army garment. There was nothing to do about it and the possibility became forgotten.

The object of paramount importance was to find the address which was so indelibly printed on my memory, consisting of a girl's name and the number and name of the street. It was difficult in a large city to find a street without asking one or maybe several people and this had a potential risk. The information available about the plan of the town in the camp was very meagre and I had no idea in what area it lay. The name of the street was not easy to pronounce and I kept repeating 'Rue de l'Europe', rolling the r's with a hopeless Anglo-Saxon accent.

Who would be the best type of person to ask? It would need to be someone reasonably intelligent, an individual, not an official, someone who, sensing the unusual, would be inclined to take no action and forget in preference to the opposite.

Having now reached the quay along the riverside I decided to make towards the docks, the most likely area to find an address of this sort. If I drew a blank it might mean searching three or four districts which would be very time-consuming and frustrating. Nearer to the docks I decided to turn down a side street and ask the first benign looking middle-aged female to appear. There were few people about but before long there came a woman in a voluminous black dress filled to capacity, a shawl round her head and shoulders, carrying a large cloth bag in her left hand.

'*Madame*.'

She stopped rather grudgingly as her thoughts switched from something absorbing to apprehend this rather uncouth-looking creature. '*Monsieur*.' 'Can you tell me where I can find the Rue de l'Europe?' 'Yes', she replied. 'You take — yes', she thought, putting her index finger to the corner of her mouth and then waving her arm there gushed forth a stream of directions that were difficult to follow, but I caught the idea. Go back to the main road by the quay, turn right and keep straight on. It was about ten minutes' walk. She obviously had some doubt of my comprehension.

'You understand?'

'Yes,' I replied.

Turning to go she hesitated to look me in the face and then continued. We walked together to the main street and when we parted in opposite directions she made no gesture of farewell. Obviously her mind was back once more to the difficulty of shopping, or whatever it was. It was a good sign.

To have hit the district first go was luck with perhaps a modicum of good deduction and this had a reassuring effect. The main road by the quay was Quai Gaston Boulet and as I walked west I took note of the names of all the side streets. A definite object and a sense of direction gave me purpose in my step and I felt less conspicuous.

The day was bitterly cold and overcast, dirty piles of snow hung about the corners and gutters and the sky looked ready at any moment to give forth another snowstorm. It was the third week in February and as yet there had been no sign of a break in the weather. The civilians looked generally grim and underfed, they walked huddled up and many of the women wore clogs. In the centre of the town there had been a sprinkling of smart women with stockings, trim shoes, handbags and hats but in the side streets shawls, black dresses and cloth bags were the predominant feature. The men looked hungry and overworked; hopelessness, frustration and fear were in their faces.

After walking fast for a quarter of an hour there above my head was a blue and white sign on the wall, Rue de l'Europe.

I crossed over the street, the house on the corner was a café and it seemed likely that this was the place of my search. I stood and looked at the café. The side street was a cul-de-sac bordered by one-storey terraced houses, no more than seventy yards long. On the door of the café was an advertisement for Dubonnet hung aslant on the window but any view into the interior was obscured by dirty lace curtains and misted glass. I pushed open the door and the vibration rang a bell. A woman was standing behind the bar and two men were leaning on it talking to her.

I glanced at the lady behind the bar and caught her eye.

'*Monsieur*.'

'*Madame*,' and touching my beret said, 'A coffee.'

'Yes, *Monsieur*.'

I selected a table in the corner away from the bar. The coffee was ambrosia, hot, black and sweet but in a disappointingly small cup made of earthenware nearly a centimetre thick. I could have sunk ten of them without noticing. With two gulps it was finished and I waited to ask for more and meanwhile sat thinking, listening to the conversation as it was parried between the two men and the woman.

The cafés in occupied France had become clubs for friends and acquaintances. Some were centres for free gossip, for passing news or airing hatred of their oppressors. Some were centres for sabotage and organised resistance. In the warmth of friendliness they would open like flowers on a midsummer day but in an instant on the entry of a strange face they would close like clams.

I decided to wait until they had gone before tackling the problem and then to make a clean breast of it alone with the woman behind the bar. There was an obvious risk. The place might now be blown and watched, in which case there would be a cold response.

'Another coffee please.'

'Yes, *Monsieur*.'

'Have you a bigger *café au lait*, I am thirsty?'

At that point the two men got up, bade her farewell and departed. The bell on the door rang and then there was silence.

'Have you any bread?'

'You have ration tickets?'

'No.'

Again there was silence, she turned round and disappeared through the open door at the back of the bar. My hopes began to rise as I slid optimistically on to a stool at the bar. She came through the door with a large cup of coffee and a hunk of bread. The joy of seeing that was unbelievable and had my mouth remained open she would have realised that I oozed gratitude. She smiled and accepted some cash and then got busy washing glasses and tidying the bottles on the shelves. Now was the moment. My mouth opened to say something, hesitated a little and then in as normal a voice as possible said, 'I have come from a prisoner of war camp and was given this address to carry in my mind.'

'Yes.' There was no sign of surprise on her face, nor of encouragement to proceed.

'The name was Colette.'

There was a short pause.

'Oh, yes, she lives in one of the houses behind the café, at No 4, but I think she is not there now.'

'When is she coming back?'

'Perhaps this afternoon.' She shrugged her shoulders.

'Do you know of any others who have been here?'

'No, I have seen none.'

Either this was the wrong place or Madame was covering up. I stood there in silence for a time and contemplated the next move. Madame was busy again with her bottles and showed no inclination to say anything more. My welcome was running out. There seemed nothing else to do but to leave.

'Thank you very much. *Au revoir, Madame.*'

'*Monsieur.*' This was said with an air of relief and it was obvious that my departure was welcome.

The bell rang once again and I was out in the cold furtively looking round for any would-be watcher and seeing nothing made a visual reconnaissance of the cul-de-sac. It was some sixty metres long with about ten terraced one-storey houses on each side. No 4 was only two doors from the café. I knocked on a dirty brass knocker, waited and there was no reply. I knocked again. There was still no answer.

'She is not there.'

A head with a purposeful expression and long, greasy, black hair had popped out from an upstairs window next door.

'When is she coming back?'

'I do not know, perhaps this evening.'

I intended to thank the lady but the head had disappeared as quickly as it had come while I was turning back through the little gate. Hopes were crashing rapidly and as I retraced my steps I sensed an aura of discouragement infiltrating the expectations that I had built up of this second haven of refuge. It was not yet hopeless but the idea of a friendly reception was fading fast. It would not pay to return within three hours and meanwhile there was little to do but keep on walking. To spend this time on the streets would be exhausting and risky.

Coming back towards the centre of the town I passed a cinema and immediately realised that this was the answer to my problem. To sit there, secluded in the dark and to go to sleep at once became an ecstatic dream. The bill outside showed Yvonne Printemps in *Les Trois Valses*. I got a ticket without any difficulty and sank into a warm comfortable seat with a feeling of complete security.

It was nearly four o'clock when I surfaced mentally and limbered myself into physical activity, left the cinema and walked back along the Avenue. The café showed more signs of life, the windows were steamed up and as I passed the door opened, the bell rang and a man came out. There was a hum of conversation from the smoky interior and a ray of warmth and friendship came forth until the door closed with a bang. I felt alone and longed to be one of them. Turning into the cul-de-sac I approached No 4 with trepidation, opened the little gate and gave the brass knocker two taps, which resounded through the little house but there was no answer. Another knock and I waited and then just as I was turning to go the door opened gently and a little old lady peered up at me from the room inside, which was a step lower than the pavement. Her face was drawn and very lined. She looked anxious and worried. She had a shawl round her head and a few untidy grey hairs hung over her forehead. Her right hand, shiny and gnarled, gripped the door knob.

As she looked up I touched my beret and said:

'*Madame*, do you know Colette?'

'Yes, she has left.'

'For a long time?'

'I do not know,' she said, looking down at the ground.

I felt sorry for the old lady and appreciated that she was reluctant to continue with the conversation holding the door open but she was the only straw I had to clutch and my need was desperate.

'*Madame*, I am an escaped prisoner of war and this address was given to me to memorise a long time ago.' With that I handed her my papers but she had no wish to see them.

'*Monsieur*,' she said, 'I understand but Colette has had to go away.' It was easy to imagine the circumstances especially as I had originally been warned that this address had been used for some time. It was probable that things had got too hot for Colette and that she had had to go elsewhere or perhaps she had already been arrested.

The little old lady stood and looked one way and another. She was anxious to close the door and her hand quivered on the knob as she pulled it a little towards her. She was frightened and glanced at intervals to the end of the street. She looked up at me with fear and sadness in her eyes and it was obvious that I had no right to detain her any longer.

'There is nothing to do, *Monsieur*,' and she shrugged her thin little shoulders in despair. The door closed carefully and slowly and the earth fell in silence around me.

Automatically I turned round back through the little gate and up the pavement to the main road, past the café, which now no longer had any interest; it was a spent attraction and had nothing to offer in the way of help. I must have passed its steamed-up windows without giving it further thought, overwhelmed by disappointment and despair. A black depression was taking charge. I was at a complete loss to know what to do, physically exhausted after walking for the greater part of four days and nights in severe winter conditions, hungry, miserable at losing Jock and frustrated at being nearly back to square one as regards getting away from my place of escape. After seven days I was no nearer home and had, it seemed, lost all prospects of getting there. Somehow I would have to get out of Rouen to find somewhere to sleep before the curfew.

Trudging back along the road to the quay, oblivious of the surroundings and the passers by, the vortex of the City drew me towards its centre. From there I had a vague idea that I would strike north, away from the bridges over the Seine, into open country, to find a haystack or a barn for the night. There was an alternative that gradually took shape. To go back to Rouen station and find a train for Paris. The liaison officer of the 12th CCS was from Paris and it was possible that he was now living at home as a civilian. Without papers I might be picked up at the barrier but in a wave of defeatism it seemed less important and recapture would at least take me off the streets and give me something to eat.

Gradually the idea of going to Paris developed and seemed to take preference to another night in the hay, where I should be no better off on the next day and would almost certainly have to come back into Rouen. The idea of staying in a hotel in Rouen was abandoned owing to the necessity of showing papers before getting the room. What to do when I got to Paris was another problem, but at least it would be well away from our area of escape and my friend's name, Theophile Pathé, was prominent in its connections with the cinema world and might be traceable without great difficulty.

The station was about three kilometres away, a walk to the quay, along the quay and then up the Boulevard Gambetta. I knew it from the morning, but the idea raised no enthusiasm in my dejected and weary state. I was poleaxed by things going wrong and haunted by the picture of the sad old lady with grey hairs blowing across her brow. There seemed to be no fundamental answer to my problem and no way out of the mess. I realised, too, that Theophile had gone to England from Dunkirk and that the chance of making contact in Paris was remote.

Walking along the quay, perhaps for the first time during the last half hour, I looked up. The sky was grey with dark clouds which the wind whipped in haste across the arc of celestial gloom. Into the clouds some 500 feet high reached the great iron spire of the cathedral and as the clouds raced past it seemed to fall backwards on to the city. The spire was set on a tower of majestic beauty from which ran the length of the roof of the nave to the west end where two other towers, quite different in design, rose in stately grandeur. It was an immense mass dominating the damaged buildings in its surround.

As I walked along the quay, almost aimlessly, my mind frozen into inanition I was conscious of the faint attraction of the station and the laborious alternative of walking out into the country. It may be that lack of enthusiasm for either turned my steps left and I found myself making for the Cathedral with no more active intent than a moth drawn to a candle.

A stillness descended upon me as I entered the great west door. The chatter and footsteps of people on the pavements, the noise of cart wheels and hooves on the cobbled streets and the hooting of cars faded into the background. The food in the shop windows was no longer there to tempt and the hum of conversation in the cafés was silenced. There were no uniforms and the eyes of the Boche were gone. The atmosphere penetrated with its stony and dignified stillness. Halfway up the centre aisle I turned between two rows of chairs and sat down at the foot of one of the main columns. I was alone but here isolation seemed to bring relief, a chance to relax and think in silence and psychologically, as it were, to hand over the problem of getting away.

Facing the nave on either side stood the massive grey pillars in purposeful dignity composedly and relentlessly supporting the burden which had been their lot for over seven hundred years. They must have witnessed, through the centuries, the cry of many who were lost and perplexed.

Tranquillity entered my being and I sank to my knees on the flag stones of the floor, my shoulders dropped and my face burrowed into my frozen hands. Tears welled up and I wept. Tension relaxed and my limbs began to come to life as I crouched in this emotive state.

Some time later I instinctively straightened, lifted my head and gazed up, up through the greyness inside the great spire and into the depth of beyond. I prayed. I had never really prayed before. I prayed with everything that I had until my mind and spirit ached that I might go back to those I loved and to my home which seemed so far away. While I prayed I believed. Belief had never really come before. While I prayed there came Faith. Faith had never come before. There was no need to try to believe nor to reach for faith.

Without thinking, without reasoning, there came an assurance, a certainty that at once gripped me in the depths of its security.

For the first time in my experience it seemed right and proper to ask for something that was essential and imminently necessary and to relax into a state of dependence and irresponsibility and passively to accept guidance. Perhaps for me there never had been anything so definite and fundamentally important to ask and hope for as there was then. As I prayed there came a sense of relief transcending any emotion that I had previously known.

It was getting dark. I gazed up to the vault of the nave and my eyes wandered along the infinite greyness. Away up there in the corners of the roof the delicate pattern of the vaulting was lost in increasing obscurity. This murky haze which clouded the roof and lurked in the corners seemed to drift along the length of the rafters towards the transepts and there sped upwards to the higher level below the great tower. I could imagine it gaining momentum as it rose up the tower and raced towards the pinnacle of the immense spire so far above. The silence was absolute but up there among the lofty masonry time seemed to stand still and the atmosphere vibrate with the code of the ages, unconcerned by the present. Far away in the east was the failing light of the window. The red lamp shone like a beacon from the sanctuary ever twinkling forth its message of peace. From the chapels on either side the little flames of candles burned bright and gutted out their communication of faith.

My heart was lifted. Slowly I recovered and sank back into the pew, remaining motionless. I was alone no longer. Gradually I felt my courage and confidence returning and sat still and let it penetrate my wretched body.

I got up, stretched my limbs and walked slowly back down the aisle. Out in the open again the hum of the city came as an equal challenge. I walked straight ahead down a narrow street full of shops and under an arch beneath a superstructure with a great clock. I was thinking hard about my next move. It was about six and getting dark and I knew there must be a curfew later in the evening and it was necessary either to get off the streets or away out into the country by then. I decided to go to the station and take a train to Paris. I could either spend the rest of the night on a bench in the station in Paris or if there was no train find a bench in Rouen station. The idea of asking anyone for help in Rouen appalled me by its potential risk to them, the old lady was still in my mind. It was necessary to turn down towards the quay and then left again along the quay to the station where I had arrived that morning. I had conveniently forgotten the military control that was examining the papers of all people leaving the station and did not know then that they were specifically looking for me.

Thus I was walking back along the Quai du Havre heading for almost certain capture. The cafés were full now as the men left their work and called in on their way home. They were busy with chatter, warm with friendship and pleasantly refreshed with aperitifs. I felt a little miserable passing their doors. I felt bedraggled and longed for the company within them and a good meal but my mind was made up and the station was my target. As I was walking along an uneasy feeling came upon me and turning sufficiently I noticed two German soldiers moving at the same pace about twenty yards behind. This made me conscious of the tear in my mack but there was nothing to do other than keep going and possibly turn down the next side street. Then there was an undoubted change in the footsteps, it seemed that someone was trying to catch me up but I dared not look round again.

As the steps came nearer and I realised that it was someone different and the person who drew level was a man of medium height with a little girl hanging on to his arm. I was unable to understand this and could not think why the person wanted to approach me but he came closer and walked by my side for a few steps. Quickly the person turned his head towards me.

'*Vous êtes anglais*?' he said, more as a statement than a question.

I was completely nonplussed by this encounter and said nothing and went on walking, taking no notice. The man with the little girl on his arm fell back and seemed hesitant as to what to do. Then almost immediately his steps quickened and he caught up again. He took my arm and repeated, 'You are English?'

'Yes.'

The unknown visitor started talking volubly. I realised what a fantastic risk he was taking and that our freedom depended on our behaviour during the next few seconds. Meeting his eye I instinctively trusted him and to my astonishment he wheeled me round past the oncoming Germans and back along the way we had come.

'You have escaped from Sotteville, haven't you?'

'Yes, how did you know?'

'I will tell you later.'

He went on talking until we were well away from the two Germans and I was dumbfounded by his audacity and speed of

Rouen Cathedral

Bernard, Lucie and Paulette Pigeon with the author at their home in Rue de Lecat. First reunion, 1944

action. I was perfectly content to be taken anywhere for there was no doubting his friendliness and sincerity. It was a complete mystery to me how I had been picked out and why it had been done. It seemed such a terrific risk to do this just under the nose of two German soldiers who were in an excellent position to see the whole procedure.

After a short walk back down the quay the unknown companion pushed open the door of a café. There was a crowd inside busy in conversation which ceased abruptly as soon as they saw me come in and all eyes turned on the stranger. My unknown companion turned towards the man behind the bar and waving his hand towards me, 'Allow me to present' and then he turned and said, 'What is your name?'

'Philip.'

'Philip, my friend, he is English.'

As a gesture I pulled out my identification card and prisoner of war disc and placed them on the bar. The Frenchman looked at them and read 'Major Philip Newman – you are a Commandant?' 'Yes.' 'My God, what a prize. I am Bernard and this is Monsieur Gabard.'

The conversation started up again and the drinks began to flow. I was given some wine and a cigarette. Bernard turned to me confidentially and said, 'You are safe here, understand? You can come home with me this evening and stay there until we find you somewhere to go.' I could only nod and say 'yes' and 'no' in what presumed to be the proper places. It was all so unbelievable. The warmth, the friendliness, the security were overwhelming. The conversation and laughter were now running high and many questions were fired at me, most of which I could not understand but it was obvious that Bernard was the hero of the night, he had landed the biggest fish and his little daughter, Paulette, sat in a corner gazing in admiration.

Soon we were on the move. Bernard walked quickly, it needed much effort to keep up with him. His head was in the air and there was purpose in his gait. Paulette ran a little and walked now on the pavement and now in the road and sometimes with one foot on the curb and the other in the gutter. Both Bernard and I were too absorbed in other things to notice the difficulty that Paulette had in keeping up. She was a little out of breath and as she panted from above a voluminous woollen scarf minute particles of ice gathered on the wool and her breath blew like steam into the freezing air. She was excited, wide-eyed, and red-cheeked in response to the rapid change of events, so much so that she wrung her hands and hugged her waist with her elbows. Frequently her father brought people home but not quite like this, not with such haste and such silence and with so complete an abandon of the usual daily events. Thus the size of the catch, its large bulk and its ungainly gait she sensed but not its real unpalatability, the potential danger of an electric eel or man-eating shark.

We turned up a narrow street, cobbled, overhung with high walls and black shapes of houses. Everything was dark except for the faint outline of the buildings against a very slight relief of the sky. The little street had the three of us to itself and half way down Bernard stopped, felt for a moment with his hand for something near his head, a catch snapped and a small door swung open.

'*Entrez*.'

It was a small opening cut within a larger gate and needed a large step to negotiate it and then I realised we were in a courtyard. An oblique path led us to a door. Bernard pushed it open into a small hall and then into a kitchen. He shut the door behind us, passed across the room and put his head round the corner of another doorway leading to what might be a scullery.

'*Chérie – rencontre Philip*.'

'*Qui*?'

'*Mon ami*.'

'*Quel ami*?'

There was a moment, an age in experience, while something was set down and a metallic door shut. A woman appeared at the door, her hands wet, her face still. She was tallish, with dark, slightly disarranged, hair, an apron tied round her waist, on which she wiped her hands. Her face at once attractive, her brow a little depressed with bewilderment but her eyes alert, kind and receptive. She paled as in a flash she realised the gravity of the onus that was falling on them but her harassed expression was as soon challenged and beaten by a smile of welcome. She brushed the hair away from her forehead with the back of her wrist.

'*Vous êtes anglais*?'

'*Oui*.'

'*C'est Philip*. He is an officer escaped from the camp for prisoners of war on the other side of the river. Philip, meet Lucie, my wife.'

Lucie smiled at me in such a confident way that it momentarily overcame all the anguish that showed in her face.

'He has come from the camp in Sotteville. The prisoners left there a few days ago. I know because I saw them going to the station under heavy guard.'

'When did you get out?'

'Just a week ago, Tuesday night to be exact. We hid in the camp for two days after they had gone and then got out.'

'Where have you been since? I cannot think why you have not been picked up before; nobody' and here Bernard's face lit up into a devilish smile 'could mistake you for a Frenchman, not even in that beret. What have you been doing for a whole week. Not wandering about Rouen?'

'No, I have been all round the country until I came back here.'

'There was someone else with you?'

'Yes, there was, but I lost my friend after two days out. I don't know where he is but I believe he was recaptured. He got ill and when I returned the next day to a rendezvous he was not there and I could get no news of him. So I came back to Rouen where I had an address to go to, but it was all over; just a very old lady who was unable to help.'

'Where were you going tonight when I picked you up?'

'To Rouen station, to get a train for Paris in the hope of finding the liaison officer of our old unit.'

'But you have no papers!' exclaimed Bernard in excitement. 'How could you have got on to the train? There is a control on each platform, they have been there ever since you escaped, looking for you.'

I began to realise how precarious was my state at the moment Bernard picked me up and what incredible fortune that my journey was cut short.

Bernard then went off into a very rapid and exhilarated conversation explaining all the details of his finding me walking along the pavement in front of the two German soldiers. Paulette sat in silence, her face alight and her hands squashed between her knees, endorsing everything that her father said with animated expressions and nods of her head. She had been there at the moment of decision and although picking me up in front of two Germans may not have seemed anything very unusual to her the incident was very rapidly increasing in drama now that she heard her father describe it. Her pride for her father was overflowing and expanded even more as she realised that it was she and not her mother who was there with him.

I sat still on a corner seat absorbing everything but the conversation, overwhelmed by a sense of security, the smell of cooking, the noise of a fire in the grate and the warmth of Lucie's smile. It was that, outshining her immediate reaction to panic, which meant so much.

'When did you last eat? Are you hungry?' And while I was still composing my answer –

'You will need some new clothes and a bed. The bed is easy, we have a spare one in the next room, but the clothes – *ou la la* – you are so big. Most Frenchmen are not big like you.' Bernard raised his head, back and shoulders as we stood up back to back, there was six inches difference.

'It is the quality that matters', came from Bernard like a whiplash.

'You cannot fit clothes to quality, *mon chéri*.'

Here we all had a laugh which relieved a lot of tension.

'You will not be able to change for supper tonight,' and at this Lucie withdrew into the scullery once more to wriggle the fire and clatter the pans.

'Have we anything worth eating for supper?' shouted Bernard. And from the scullery came a reply which I was to hear so often during the next few weeks: '*Y a rien, rien, rien.*'

'I have been shopping most of the day and could only get a few artichokes and some bread. What have you brought with you?'

'A bottle of wine.'

'I'm sure. Is that all?'

'No.'

'What else?'

'A British soldier.'

'Fool.'

And then coming to the scullery door, Lucie looked at me.

'You must excuse my husband, he gets childish at times – we are not cannibals – sometimes shopping gets a little difficult but so far we have not deteriorated lower than horse meat and shellfish, we still have cats and rats in reserve.'

I was perfectly content to sit still and marvel at their repartee born from adversity. Their home, with me behind the front door, was now a potential sword of Damocles with Bernard in the chair.

Bernard and Paulette had disappeared out through the front door and I sat there wondering what a fourth mouth would mean to their rations. How short were their supplies, how hungry were they? During the last twenty months I had experienced so many degrees of hunger ranging from very little to barely enough. These degrees of hunger had at times been relieved by Red Cross parcels and parcels from other sources, a service of inestimable value to the prisoner of war, not only for the food but as a bargaining value of primary importance. I did not know yet what I was in for but I was in no way worried by the prospect of another period on short rations. I was much more concerned on the element of danger that I brought and the diminishing effect on their rations, because there was nothing that I could do about it apart from providing some money.

In a few minutes Bernard and Paulette were back. Bernard carried some paper in his left hand. He put it on the table and unwrapped it, there were four small pieces of sausage and from his coat pocket he produced two oranges.

'*Voilà*,' said he, throwing his hands into the air. '*C'est quelque chose.*'

'What have you got?' said Lucie emerging from the scullery with a saucepan in her hand. Paulette stood by the table and beamed and the three stood there looking for a moment.

'What a meal! Who gave you these?'

'Marie.'

'How kind of her. You have told her then.'

'Yes, she had to know.'

Lucie paled, took a deep breath and returned to her cooking.

Bernard was like a child with a new toy. He went next door and returned with four or five excited people who came into the little room. At first there was silence as they listened to Bernard introducing his strange visitor and then much hand shaking, friendly smiles and nodding approvals as the story unfolded in all its glory. Amid exclamations and questions my history came out in halting French but insufficiently embellished for Bernard who frequently interrupted with his own additions. Each pair of eyes was on us and each face radiated an expression of amazement and admiration.

The conversation mounted in vivacity and speed far beyond the original narrative into a spate of extravagant whims and imaginations indicating the temporary relief of frustration and tension that this episode was providing.

The excitement gradually subsided as they realised that Lucie was waiting to serve the meal and that it was not for them. There was a lot more hand-shaking before they returned next door.

We eventually sat down to eat at nine o'clock at a round table in the middle of the kitchen. The meal started with some soup which could be distinguished from hot water by a gentle brown tint and a few pieces of cabbage leaf in temporary suspension. There followed some artichokes covered with a white sauce created with a touch of culinary art which made them deliciously insufficient. The four pieces of sausage looked very naked lying alone on a serving plate as Lucie carefully set them on to the centre of the table.

Here originated a pattern of procedure which was to be repeated throughout the three weeks that I was their lodger. Always Bernard, who was at this time undoubted master in the household, would say, '*Servez-vous, Philip.*' My hesitation was at once overruled and no one moved until I had obeyed this generous and affectionate order. With the sausage came a few *haricots verts*, a glass of *vin ordinaire* and a slice of bread. The meal was concluded with half an orange.

Any attempt to help with the washing up was immediately squashed by Bernard who conveyed to me in one word and a very purposeful expression that that was just not the sort of thing a man should do.

The conversation during the meal had been a repeat of the evening's events in greater detail, describing my kidnapping in front of the two German soldiers, exactly where it had happened and the explanation to and the reaction of those in the Café des Belges on the Quai du Havre. Lucie wanted to know all about the characters who were there and their individual reactions.

Then Bernard turned round and spoke slowly to me, explaining that the café was a de Gaulle centre, that everyone knew each other and felt free to say what they wished until an unknown face came in the door. This I easily understood but found his other rapid patter in vernacular difficult to follow. I was perfectly content to sit there in silence watching their animated features and the play of expression on their faces.

Bernard had got one back on the Boche which gave him great satisfaction. I was to learn later that he had to work for them for a living but hated their guts. He was a motor mechanic and his garage had been taken over by the Wehrmacht and he spent his time servicing and repairing army vehicles. This he explained to me while the ladies were washing the dishes in the scullery. Lucy, he told me, mended German uniforms and he drew a curtain behind where we were sitting, to show many hanging in a cupboard. He explained that Germans at any time during the day were likely to bring or collect their goods and although they very seldom came into the house I would have to be careful not to be too obvious. Fortunately their house was in a courtyard with five others and he reminded me of coming in through a small gate in a large double door in order to get into the courtyard. This small gate was the only entrance for all six houses.

Lucie had finished her dishes and then was prepared to discuss the very important matter of accommodation. They took me up the little staircase. There was one medium-sized room where Bernard and Lucie slept and a small room belonging to Paulette. I was allotted Paulette's room and she very generously agreed to her mother's suggestion that she slept in the alcove separated from the kitchen by a curtain.

Bernard took me into his bedroom and showed me a door which led into a storage space under the roof. There was no need to tell me that here was the place of retreat if the necessity arose. Ample room was available behind the boxes and stored furniture and there was no light from outside. The bedrooms had attic windows in the roof with lace curtains and they faced the high brick wall of the road side of the courtyard so that no one could see in.

The beds were soon made up. 'You must be tired,' Bernard said to me and then before bidding me goodnight he said: 'In the morning it is best for you to stay in bed until we have planned the day. It is Sunday so there will be no German callers but there may well be some friends and we shall have to decide who is and who is not to know.' My orders were clear and could be discharged without any hardship.

I said goodnight to Lucie, Paulette and Bernard and in some very inadequate words attempted to say how much I appreciated all that they had done, but they and I knew that what had been done for me that evening was beyond words and undoubtedly there was much more to come. The emotion of the moment passed like a damp squib but our smiles bridged the gap of seeping apprehension.

'*Bon soir, Philip. Dormez bien.*'

'*Et vous aussi.*'

I climbed the stairs and got into bed. Warm, fed and secure, sleep should have come as an inevitable response but the reverse was the case.

Then memory of my grandmother came to me. She used to take me to Church as a small boy and had given me a present, on my eighth birthday. It was a Bible and in the cover she had written, 'Ask and it shall be given you'.

That was exactly what had happened and it kept my mind wondering for much of the night.

When I woke in the morning I recalled that the orders were to stay in bed until the plans for the day had been completed. This was one of the easiest orders it had ever been my lot to obey. In warmth and comfort sleep came again.

Some time towards the end of the morning I was woken by the sound of voices downstairs. There were quite a few people it seemed and lots of excited, semi-hushed chatter, which had no difficulty in taking over the little house.

I heard somebody coming upstairs and Bernard appeared at the door with an armful of garments.

'Our friends have made a search for clothes. So will you do your best with them, turn yourself into a Frenchman and come down and meet everyone.'

'You know very well that you are asking the impossible but I will do my best. You must have been up early this morning.'

'Yes, at seven o'clock,' he replied.

I was thankful for his order of the previous evening, it relieved all sense of guilt.

'*Alors*,' concluded Bernard, turning around quickly and departing downstairs.

I spread all the various things out and had an interesting five minutes or so trying to create a *tout ensemble*, but it was not easy.

In considerable trepidation I went slowly downstairs to be confronted with a sudden lull in the conversation and many looks of intense enquiry. Bernard came to my rescue and presented me as Philip and I shook everyone by the hand.

We sat down nine round the table and all the chatter recommenced. I engaged my two neighbours in a short conversation which was obviously very little understood and very soon they broke back into the general repartee and interchange which was not to be missed. For these people Sunday lunch was the big occasion of the week to foregather and pass round the news since the previous time. It soon became obvious that this was a circle of very close friends, prepared to discuss anti-German activities in open conversation and together leading a life of potential danger. That day Bernard was their hero with Lucie and Paulette in close association. I gathered that someone known to them all had been shot that week for hiding weapons in his garage.

Lunch was a pool of various dishes brought by them all. There seemed to be plenty of beans and bread, a very adequate foundation to any meal.

Not until late in the afternoon did the circle start to break up, leaving behind it a very well used atmosphere and a pile of washing up.

I knew from experience the evening before that my help with clearing or washing up was definitely not acceptable. As a counter-attraction Bernard took me aside and showed me something which was obviously precious and hidden in a secret place. It was a Cross of Lorraine, the emblem of their Service. They were one group of many de Gaulle circles and their headquarters was the Café des Belges.

More and more I realised my great fortune in being salvaged by a member of such a band.

Bernard explained to me the outcome of their discussion from which I had gleaned some of the points, but by no means all. It was their plan to get me proper French papers, complete with a photo, so as to convert me into a fellow countryman in that there would be something to show when challenged during travel. When my papers were ready it would be possible to go south by train to the neighbourhood of the Demarcation line. Meanwhile I was to stay with them.

As I had no alternative plan there was little else to do but accept. They had obviously chewed over the possibilities during the afternoon and come to this conclusion. The burden it imposed on Bernard and Lucie was immense.

Had I walked out that night Lucie would have been relieved of an extra mouth to feed on a meagre supply and Bernard spared the haunting risk of a skeleton in the cupboard but their reaction would inevitably have been one of frustration and anger that the fruits of such a hazardous endeavour had been cast aside. 'Never again' they would have said. I was their fish and they would not appreciate my jumping out of the basket back into the river. I had no answer but to accept this priceless offer, lie low and do as I was told.

'*Vous comprenez?*'

'*Oui, oui, mais quelquechose formidable pour vous.*'

'*N'importe, c'est un grand plaisir.*'

The evening passed. Paulette sat in a corner learning her catechism. This was her year of confirmation and I was impressed by the concentrated study that had been going on for over an hour.

Some time later her father decided to hear her recite some pieces. This she attempted very nervously in a halting flow of response. At first she coped reasonably well with some prompting from her father but later seized up in abject fear.

Perhaps the events of the last two days had modified her concentration or the presence of a stranger caused embarrassment but in retrospect it was more likely she sensed that the cone had been hoisted for a gale warning. She was given little allowance for these potential excuses by Bernard. He was obviously very unimpressed by her efforts and after minutes of mounting criticism concluded the hearing by throwing the book at her.

It was a dramatic climax and an embarrassing situation for all of us but probably more so for me who had come from a family unacquainted with the art of emotional discharge in that sort of way. Paulette screamed and then wept in deep extended sobs, her mother retreated into the scullery and I hung my head with an expressionless mask of neutral concern on my face.

More quickly than would seem possible the tension ebbed away. Bernard and Lucie were soon back to discussing some delicate arrangements for the next day and Paulette, realising that the effect of her emotive reaction to fear and injustice had passed, picked up the book and resumed her preparation for the next encounter.

Monday morning came. I heard Bernard get up and go at an early hour but very quickly realised that there was nothing to do except lie quiet and keep out of the way. I had noticed in the bookcase downstairs some volumes of the history of the last war. It was the main feature in its shelves and I realised that this would be an admirable pastime. It would keep me quiet in one chair, improve my French and in addition be a fascinating interest to read the history of the war from a French angle. In the middle of the morning I crept downstairs and put my head round the corner. Lucie was busy with the German uniforms, there was steam rising from the damp cloth as she pressed hard with the iron. She looked up and beckoned me to a chair.

'*Vous avez bien dormi*?'

'*Oui, et vous*?'

'*Très bien – merci*.'

When the ironing was finished Lucie disappeared into the scullery and I used that moment to observe the optimum position to sit. It was fortunate that anyone approaching the front door from outside had first to enter the main courtyard gate and then pass down a path about twenty yards long. I placed my chair so that I could see the main gate and the adjoining part of the path and would rely on being alered by the rather noisy catch of the small door within the large gate. It was important to sit well back in the room so that anyone approaching down the path could not see me.

Lucie came back with a cup of coffee and a piece of bread, set it down beside me and explained that it was not much but better than nothing. It seemed an appropriate moment to discuss my plan with her explaining that I would spend my time reading the history of the war and sit in a position so as to watch the gate and that I would disappear upstairs whenever anyone entered the compound.

There was silence while she digested my schoolboy French and a plan of designed inactivity. Sitting in a chair away from the window with a view of the front gate while I read the history of the war seemed to appeal to her but the idea of racing upstairs whenever anybody came to the front door was not accepted with such favour.

She explained that no German ever came inside the house but I was not happy with the security. The front door opened into one end of the main room and although there was a curtained-off rectangle inside the room, making it impossible to see into the interior, it seemed nevertheless too intimate a situation for repeated practice.

Within half an hour the front gate into the courtyard clicked and there stepping over the lower plank was a German private. Within a moment I slipped upstairs and stood on the landing with a very good view through the lace curtains. There was a knock on the front door, a few moments' conversation and then he disappeared through the main gate with an officer's uniform on his arm.

It was a very simple procedure. Lucie showed no disapproval and from then onwards it became a routine except on two or three occasions when I had dozed off over the history of the French army in action.

There were times when Lucie went out shopping and I was left alone in the house. On these occasions I always adjourned upstairs in case a caller, getting no response by knocking, peered into the inevitably lead to suspicion and possible verbal contact.

Shopping was a very frustrating business as there was no proper rationing system. Lucie would return sometimes after half the morning away having walked miles hunting the markets and shops and getting practically nothing. She would arrive back home completely exhausted, put what little she had got on the table and throwing her arms into the air would say, '*Y a rien, rien, rien.*'

Paulette came back from school in the late afternoon and Bernard in the evening, sometimes with a little food from sympathetic friends or from the canteen of the factory where he was employed. Lucie then would bring her undoubted culinary genius into action and create a meal out of potatoes, turnips or other oddments in the way of flavouring matter from her reserve in the cupboard. It was always wholesome and good to taste.

The next weekend we spent Sunday with friends who had a more ready access to food. The meal, a potentially frugal provision but blown up with ample beans, lasted for four hours and for the first time for two weeks I got enough to feel satisfied.

After the meal the men withdrew into a huddle and beckoned me to join the circle. It was explained that my papers were being prepared but that a photo was needed for completion. It was suggested that I should go to a store tomorrow morning and get one taken.

When we got home Bernard drew a street plan of how to get there and told me the exact price so that there would be no need for conversation.

There was no difficulty in finding the 'Monoprix' but a queue of seven or eight people sitting waiting for the machine was an embarrassment. I decided to buy a paper so as to avoid conversation and all went well until I got to the head of the queue. The attendant supervising the machine came up to me with a slight smile on his face to ask for the money but to my horror he spoke in English. I paid the money and thanked him in French, hoping that my neighbour had not noticed, but the exposure was a severe shock and not conducive to relaxed photography. I was very thankful to get out of the store with the photos secure in my pocket, not until I was again in the street mingling with the crowd could I hyponotise myself into resuming French transformation.

After three long hair-raising weeks for the Pigeon family things eventually fell into line for departure. The circle had found some clothes for travelling including a jacket, knee breeches and a beret, a small attache case with some food in it, my rail ticket to the south and papers for Henri Boseaux with my stamped photo included. Henri Boseaux was a name with an address in the telephone directory whom the circle knew no longer lived in France. The fictitious character was a male nurse going to see his sick mother in the south of France.

The ticket was to Châtellerault and on Saturday evening, 14th March, Bernard gave it to me in a nonchalant way as if it was something that came up with the rations but I was conscious that this was the ticket of release for the family, it was the final token of the completion of, for them, a very dangerous undertaking.

The train was to depart from Station de l'Ouest, Rive Droite, about 11 a.m. on Sunday morning and the obvious thing to expect was that having made sure that I knew where the station was, got my papers and my ticket that they would say goodbye at their house and I would make my way to the station. I imagined that the family and friends would then sit down and celebrate a job well done with a communal lunch as was their custom on a Sunday.

How wrong I was. Eleven people walked with me all the way from 17, Rue de Lecat to the station, a distance of barely two kilometres via the Boulevard Jeanne d'Arc. Arriving at the station the party all stood round in a circle happily talking and joking.

'Philip,' said Bernard, 'that is your train,' pointing to platform six. I was happy to see that there was no German control at the platform, just a French ticket collector, but there were a few unpleasant looking military police in parts of the station.

The *moment critique* had come. We all strolled towards the platform and I kissed or shook hands with everyone and then turning round, with rouge still on my cheek, presented the ticket collector with my ticket. It was clipped and I was through the barrier without any trouble. Soon I was walking backwards and waving to all my friends remaining in a cluster behind the ticket collector. Enough, I thought, turning and walking straight for the carriage. At a last glimpse I saw them wandering away.

What a send off! What courage! What a finale to a job perfectly executed! The slightest turn of luck or action causing suspicion could have been disastrous resulting in the usual penalty for civilians caught aiding the British – death or concentration camp. The memory of that farewell is still vivid – it was the perfect curtain.

CHAPTER SEVEN

Through France

The warmth and affection and the background apprehension, the kisses, hand-shakes and *au revoirs* gradually faded into the past as the train got further and further south and the future began to take shape. It centred around one address, which had been thrown in by a friend of Bernard, as a sure way of crossing the Demarcation Line which separated occupied from unoccupied France. The village was north of Châtellerault and he had given me the name of the farmer.

By now the name of the village and of the farmer were deeply rooted in my mental plan of action but unfortunately the donor had not impressed me with confidence so that there was an element of doubt in what to expect.

Everyone had to change at Le Mans and there was a long wait so that the time of arrival at Tours was too late for any hope of getting to the farm that day. It meant a night on the bench in the waiting room. There was nothing unusual about this in wartime France. The benches were hard but secure. They were free and very handy for catching a train and keeping abreast with local changes of times.

In the morning there was a train to Châtellerault stopping at all stations. The last before Châtellerault was close to the village and I had been told to get off there.

Confidence reached its peak when the village was where he had described and hope of finding the farm became a reality.

Behind the bar of the most obvious café in the centre of the village was a friendly looking chap, tall with a large bushy moustache, red face and receding hair. There were three men at one table, each with a *café cognac*, in deep discussion sufficiently distracting for them to appear to take no notice of my entrance.

I ordered a *vin rouge* and stood there at the counter making a few preliminary remarks about the weather and the signs of Spring waiting for a moment to pose the loaded question.

'I wonder if you could help me. I am trying to find a farmer called Clairmont.'

My host hesitated and while he thought I mentioned the name

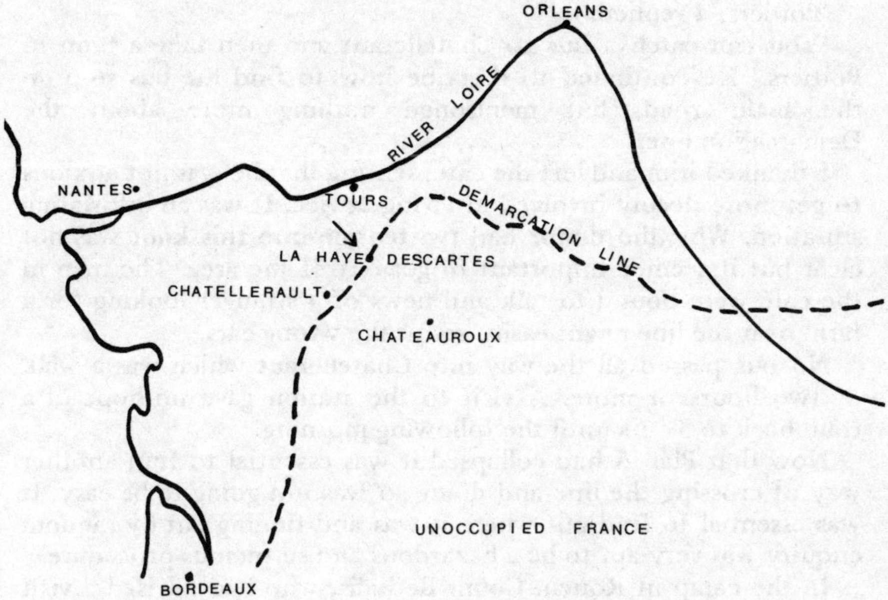

of the farm. He repeated to himself the name and then looked me straight in the face and very definitely said:

'There is no one of that name that farms in this village.' He shouted across to the three men who reluctantly stopped arguing.

'Do you know a chap called Clairmont?'

There were a few moments of contemplation followed by a unanimous decision in the negative. That was that and it seemed important to change the conversation but my host had got interested and determined to ferret it out a bit further.

'Why did you want to find him?'

'He is a friend of a friend of mine in Rouen and he suggested that I call and see him during a stay near here.'

'You are sure you have the right village.'

'That is the name he gave me. He said it was near the Demarcation line.'

'The Demarcation line – that is not here. It is ten kilometres away. You have the wrong village.'

'It must be a name very similar,' I said for the want of anything better to say, but in my heart it was an obvious diddle and my original suspicion well founded.

'Where are you making for now?' he asked.

'Poitiers,' I replied.

'You can catch a bus to Châtellerault and then take a train to Poitiers.' He continued to describe how to find the bus stop on the main road, but mentioned nothing more about the Demarcation line.

I thanked him and left the café, sensing that he was not anxious to get more deeply involved in giving advice. It was an infuriating situation. Why the donor had twisted me into this knot was not clear but it seemed important to get out of the area. The men in the café were bound to talk and news of a stranger looking for a farm near the line might easily get to the wrong ears.

No bus passed all the way into Châtellerault which was a walk of two hours or more. A visit to the station gave no hope of a train back to Tours until the following morning.

Now that Plan A had collapsed it was essential to find another way of crossing the line and doing so was not going to be easy. It was essential to find out where it was and finding out by random enquiry was very apt to be a hazardous and suspicious procedure.

In the camp in Rouen, Count de Salis, who had advised a visit to his relatives in Beaumont-le-Roger, had also told me of a great friend of his who had a bookshop in Tours. He had torn out a small map of Tours from a directory giving me an exact idea of where it was and had also given me a personal note to his friend. Plan B was taking shape. It was important to get back to Tours and to ask this chap where the line was and any advice he had to offer about crossing it.

During the course of the evening I got into a café which was noisy and full, probably a popular spot for the local lads. A group near me were not admirers of the Germans and glanced at me from time to time to note my reaction to some of their obviously audible remarks. They seemed to be reassured because their conversation became less and less camouflaged from its natural tendency.

After another wine I drew closer and got involved in actively listening and laughing and later in talking. It was a possible chance of finding out something about the line and so as not to make it too obvious I asked if it was possible to get a bus to Le Blanc, a place I guessed was on the other side.

'Le Blanc! It is the other side of the line. You have a pass?'

'No,' I said.

'It is not possible to get there without a pass.'

'How far is the line?'

ht) Airey Neave

ow) Post-war reunion of the
ers of the 12th Casualty
ring Station

A reunion thirty years later, 1972. The author with Bernard

Bernard, Anne Newman, Lucie, the author, Paule

There was no direct reply to this. One or two shrugged their shoulders and someone said, 'Between here and Le Blanc.'

'Where are you from?' one of them asked.

'From the North,' I said, realising that the conversation had gone far enough, possibly too far.

There was a lull and then the conversation drifted back to local topics and antigoonery. It was obvious that my question had caused a check and might have started something to my advantage or disadvantage.

I sat there in silence, finished off my drink and then crept out, conscious that no good was coming of it. I had broken one of the fundamental rules of escaping. However bleak and lonely the circumstances do not get involved in drinking parties with strangers. It had been the undoing of so many.

The immediate problem was to find a bed for the night. Walking through the town I came to a bridge over a river and continued on out into the country beyond for about a kilometre. Some little distance from the gate into a field a barn was dimly visible. It was not long before it became the selected site for a night's doss.

By dawn any hope of further sleep had disappeared. It was a bright morning and looking across the fields to the town a thin square tower of a church jutting above the other buildings on the west side of the river was conspicuous in the sunlight.

There were four hours to kill before the train left for Tours and going to Mass seemed a very happy answer to the problem, a God-sent gift in fact.

The church stood a block of houses away from the river and was partially surrounded by a garden with high hedges and shrubs. Down by the river was a suitable secluded spot for a wash and brush up and I managed to have a bit of a shave.

In church there were about twenty or so people, mostly mature women dressed in black and three or four men all obviously elderly. Being in there amongst them gave a feeling of relaxation and security and provided somewhere quiet to sit and think. The service went on for some time as others drifted in and out.

When it was all over the church emptied and the priest left through a curtain behind the altar. I was alone on my knees. All was quiet, all was still, and my mind went back to Rouen, the feeling of utter hopelessness which had suddenly been converted into the love and warmth of a family by one man's intuition and courage. Where had that flash of instinct come from and what had it to do with my call to the cathedral. My thoughts dwelt on that wonderful evening and my prayers were of thankfulness and for guidance.

I left by a side door. It was by then a lovely sunny morning, an inviting opportunity to go and sit by the river and eat something out of my haversack.

After a little nourishment I must have dozed off into semi-consciousness but not for long. Perhaps something alerted me but on looking up I saw a man in uniform coming down the road along the river looking at me intently. Clutching my haversack I was across the road into the small street leading to the church in a few seconds and running as fast as possible. It was about a hundred yards to the T-junction at the corner of the block and before turning I looked back and saw my pursuer enter the street and break into a run. There were a few moments. What luck that I had been to Mass that morning and used the side door. I dashed between two bushes, through the door which was ajar and across the church which fortunately was still empty and lay panting on the floor beneath a pew, my ears cocked for the sound of boots on stone. None came, but a few minutes later someone entered the porch of the main door. Moving a little it was possible to get a glimpse of the legs under the pews. It was him.

He wandered around the west end and then up the aisle to the sanctuary. It seemed certain he would find me. All he had to do was to get down on his knees and look under the pews but he just wandered back again, giving the impression that he was convinced that he had missed his game outside and did not really expect to find me in the church. He left by the main door, apparently having satisfied himself with such a perfunctory search that I was not there.

Once more the church was empty and peace reigned. The side door was still ajar and the birds' songs penetrated with a spring-time richness. I lay there with my head on my arm, lost in wonder.

There was no point in moving unless fresh footsteps sounded on the stone. Should my pursuer return there was nothing to do but lie still and pray. For anyone else it would be possible to slip into the kneeling position having appeared to be looking for something on the floor. The longer the chap who was looking for me had to get out of the district the better.

Half an hour later someone came in the main door and I could see a skirt. She walked up the aisle towards the vestry and disappeared behind a curtain. Assuming she was someone to do with the church it was a good time to leave.

I slipped out of the side door and made north through the rest of the town on the *rive gauche*. To cross the bridge back into the town for the railway station was far too risky.

It seemed wise to avoid the road for some distance and to try and get onto a bus further on. I slipped off my mack and beret and stuffed them into my haversack so as to appear, at a distance, to be a different person. About two kilometres further on I picked up a bus for Dange.

The little map of Tours, which showed only the main streets, was helpful and a sufficient guide to find the place. Suddenly, in all its glory, there it was, a bookshop with the name over the door. It was a great joy to find it.

Inside was a young lady in a white blouse and blue skirt, keen to know the nature of my enquiry.

'Is Monsieur Blois in?'

'I will see,' and she left to go through a door at the back of the shop, soon to emerge again with a middle-aged man behind her. He had a benign, intelligent face which showed an element of curiosity as he came towards me.

'Monsieur Blois?' I asked.

'Yes,' he said, with some hesitation.

'I have a personal note for you,' and I handed him this small folded piece of paper which had been hanging round my neck for so long.

He took it into the back room and in a few moments called me in and shook me warmly by the hand.

'You are from Tony de Salis. How is he? I heard he was badly wounded.'

A description of the wound and a reassurance that it was now all healed gave him great pleasure and then of course he wanted to know where he was. He listened to a description of the so-called repatriation party and the camp in Rouen where we were together and to the unfortunate news that it had now been moved back to Germany.

'So you refused to go back,' he said. 'Tony was a good friend, he was a great reader and I used to enjoy his company very much.'

'He had a flowing tongue. We used to enjoy lying on our bunks listening to him talk. He could speak excellent German and was very useful in dealing with the goons.'

'What can I do for you?' he asked.

'My object at present is to cross the Demarcation line and it would be very valuable to know just where it is.'

He at once got out a local map and without any difficulty drew the line on it.

'Your best plan is to take a bus towards La Haye-Descartes but get off before you are there. I am afraid I have no detailed knowledge to help you across. There is a German patrol line and a French line with a no-man's land in between. La Haye-Descartes is about fifty-five kilometres from here. It is the local headquarters for the frontier guards and is full of Germans. Get off the bus before you get there,' he repeated, 'because they are very liable to ask for papers of everyone getting off at a terminus. You can find the bus at the station,' and he described how to get there.

'Have you any papers in case they ask for them?'

Proudly I showed him my card.

'Henri Boseaux,' he exclaimed with a laugh. 'That is excellent. How did you come by that?'

'From my friends in Rouen.'

'I hope you get across the line safely.'

'Would you go north or south of Descartes?' I asked.

'I don't know. I have had no cause to go near the line and in conversation we avoid talking about it in case someone is suspicious. I am sorry to be so useless.'

'Thank you very much. You have given me wonderful help.'

Then, just as the moment came to say farewell a thought occurred to him.

'Would you like some money?'

It was a superb idea and there seemed no point in refusing his offer.

'That would be most helpful,' I said.

He disappeared into a back office and returned with an envelope. He pressed it into my hand and squeezed both my hands very firmly.

'I hope that will see you home.'

It was a very touching moment. We walked together to the front door and then said goodbye.

'Remember you go to the station for the bus,' was his final remark. A few moments later I turned round to wave. He was still at the door.

There was no difficulty in finding the bus but all seats were taken and packages and bundles hampered the gangway. As this noble vehicle set off it was a matter of finding foot-room and holding tight as it trundled along at a moderate pace, making heavy grinding work of the hills.

Some time later it stopped for about the twelfth time. Two nuns got off and I decided to follow suit. There was not a lot of light left to find a place for the night and hunger was gnawing my vitals.

After a short walk on the right of the road there was a lane which could be a private approach to a farm. It was. The end of the lane was closed by a large gate before opening out into a farmyard. There was a farmhouse with a smoking chimney and several sheds. One had an open door and a pile of straw, an inviting spot for the night.

I knocked on the door of the farmhouse. After a minute or so it was opened by a man with a whiskery face. He held the door only half open, looked me in the face and asked what I wanted.

'Would it be possible for me to sleep in your barn tonight?'

He hesitated and turned round. Behind him was a woman. She came to the door and said, 'Who are you?'

'I am a prisoner of war escaped from Germany.'

She glanced at her husband who had now a very worried look and was obviously averse to taking any action.

'Come in,' she said. 'I expect you are hungry. We are just going to have a meal,' and she pointed to a chair at the table.

'Put your haversack over there and come and sit down.'

Her black hair was done up in a bun. She wore an apron and her sleeves were short above the elbows. Her expression was one of determined resolve to allay the obvious doubt of her husband that such action was wise. There were two children, a boy and a girl of about twelve to fourteen, already seated at the table. Their faces were full of wonder at what was happening and reflected the state of tension that had fallen on this family circle.

The fire glowed from the stove and round the ceiling were several hams hanging from the beams. Gradually her husband accepted the decision and took his place at the table and within a short time we all had a large plate of soup and a piece of bread.

Conversation did not flow during the meal but the food did. The soup was plentiful and followed by a luscious piece of boiled ham with a varied choice of vegetables which were dished up from hot pots on the stove. When the meal was over the husband disappeared through the outside door and the two children through an inner door so that Madame and I were alone in the kitchen. She was busy clearing the table and washing up.

'You are English?'

'Yes,' I said, 'from a German camp and I am going to try and cross the Demarcation line to get to Toulouse. Here are all my papers and my prisoner of war disc if you would care to see them.'

She came over and looked at them carefully and then took me to the window. 'You can sleep in that barn. You will be all right there and no one will come in.'

'Thank you very much for taking me in and for that wonderful meal which will last me for a long time.'

She went out of the door to look round. 'It is all clear for you to go now and I hope you will have a good night.'

In the barn was a heap of straw and two carts. The most obvious thing was to make a straw bed in one of the carts to avoid the rats and other creepy crawlies that were bound to inhabit these seemly quarters.

What luck to have hit such a place at such a moment. It had solved the problem until dawn but I was no further with any plan about the line, whether to go straight into Descartes or to probe the country north or south was a decision for tomorrow. It was unfair to expect any more help from this farm situated so close. There might even have been German lodgers there and my conscience was not exactly clear at the thought of having knocked them up. There was nothing to do at that moment but to go to sleep and that came very soon.

It was not the dawn or a cock crowing that woke me, it was Madame. 'Wake up,' she said and shook my foot. 'You can come to the kitchen for a shave and some breakfast and then I will tell you where to go.'

It was difficult to believe this new development but as before she had shown herself master of the situation and it would have been crazy not to follow her lead.

A wash and a shave, a large bowl of *café au lait* with plenty of home-made bread and butter was a morale booster. Madame was busy about the kitchen and there was no conversation. No other members of the family appeared.

My hostess took two pieces of bread, spread something between them and wrapped the sandwich in paper which she put in my haversack. Then purposefully, as if she was carrying out a daily routine, she came and sat at the table.

'Listen carefully,' she said. 'It is important that you understand. You leave here and walk down the lane where you came in and turn right on the main road which goes to Descartes. It will take you about two hours. A man to whom I will introduce you outside, will leave here an hour later riding a bicycle with your haversack on his shoulder. He will catch you up and pass you as you are approaching the town. A little way ahead he will get off his bicycle and push it. Watch him carefully because he will drop your haversack inside a low gate of a house with a small front garden and cycle away. You go into that gate and knock at the front door. It will be answered by an old lady and she will let you in.'

'That is very clear. Thank you.'

Madame took me outside and there was a fine-looking old lad in a beret and rugged dark suit with his trousers tucked into his socks. He had a red, happy face with a bushy grey moustache.

'This is Simon,' said Madame and we shook hands. She showed me his bicycle which was leaning against the porch.

'He knows that you will take no notice of him as he passes you but will watch him carefully after he dismounts.'

The old boy looked at me and smiled and nodded and gave a little demonstration of passing one hand over the other and shaking his head. I assured him that his plan was understood.

Madame listened for a moment and then wished me luck. She turned into the porch and disappeared and that was the last we saw of each other.

I saluted Simon, said '*au revoir*' and set off. It was a lovely morning for walking and after a good supper, a night's sleep and a breakfast it was all pleasure, with time to think about the next move. There was little to contemplate because after meeting the old lady at her front door the important next move was wrapped in mystery.

By midday the outlying houses of Descartes were approaching and looking round I could see no sign of Simon.

There was doubtless plenty of time but instinctively my steps became a little slower and looking round was obviously to be rationed to a minimum. The main road turned and soon there were houses on either side which made me increasingly aware of my complete dependence on Simon's appearance. If he did not appear soon I should have to turn round and go back the same way. Then to my joy there was a pedalling noise behind me and slowly in a dignified manner Simon passed without a sign of recognition. After thirty yards or so he pretended to be trying to see the numbers on the doors and got off his bike and pushed it.

There were a few people about and one in uniform looked suspiciously German.

Further on Simon passed a curved row of terraced houses;

they had strips of garden in front and he stopped at one, stabilised the pedal of his bicycle against the edge of the pavement and pretended to be getting close to see the number on the door. My haversack, hanging from his left forearm was surreptitiously allowed to slip the other side of the low wall. He was soon on his bike and away. It had not obviously been noticed by anyone but it seemed a wise precaution to go on walking past the house into the town and come back.

Later I pushed open the gate and knocked on the front door. It was indeed answered by an old lady. She was tall and thin and wore a long grey dress with little black shoes. She had a sweet expression and said quite simply:

'You wish to come in?'

'Thank you,' I said.

Behind her was another old lady. They could have been twins and both possibly over eighty.

'This is my sister, Marion.'

'Call me Henri,' I said.

The front door was closed and we passed down a corridor into a room which looked out on to a fair-sized garden.

At a signal from the sister who had answered the door we sat down.

'You are English, I believe.'

'Yes, I was captured in Dunkirk two years ago.'

'Madame told me that she had seen your papers.'

'You have seen Madame?'

'Mayard! Yes, she came here last night after you had gone to bed.'

I was astounded and could do nothing but sit there and marvel that these two old dears had got involved in my welfare.

The other sister said: 'We shall be having lunch soon and I hope that there will be enough for you to eat.'

Both got up and busied themselves with cooking and preparing for the meal which quite naturally, it would seem, took precedence over anything else.

As we sat down an old boy appeared and was introduced as 'my brother'. His walking was unsteady and he leant heavily on two sticks. He was hard of hearing and could have been even older than his sisters.

While we were waiting for the meal and both the ladies were in the kitchen he seized the opportunity to tell me about La Haye-Descartes, the birthplace of the famous philosopher, mathematician and scientist, known by some as the father of modern philosophy. He had lived in a house nearby and his mother had died when he was an infant. In his prime, three hundred years ago, he was a person of originality of thought and great mental vigour. René Descartes travelled widely but finally settled in Holland to live a quiet life and to develop his fundamental association of philosophy and science with mathematics.

Just as this old companion was really enjoying himself opening up on his favourite subject the soup arrived and he looked crestfallen.

The conversation changed to small talk by the sisters. One of them explained to me that after lunch it would be possible to rest and sleep in the drawing room during the afternoon until Pierre arrived to tell me what to do. This was the first suggestion that there was any further plan beyond this house and its three charming inhabitants.

Most of the furniture in the drawing room was covered by dust sheets but one settee had been cleared and two folded rugs and a pillow had been placed there for my comfort. There were many busts and statues to share my transcendency into a bygone age but lying there struck me as a very odd preparation for crossing the line and my sense of purpose bubbled with impatience and frustration.

It was a great relief when the elder sister called me out into the garden. There was a young lad of about sixteen or seventeen who was introduced as Pierre.

My hostess explained with pride that he looked after their garden and that they were lucky to have him. Pierre smiled and stood there in silence. He wore no hat over a shock of unkempt light brown hair. His expression was one of sincerity and basic understanding with a constant potential of humorous appreciation.

'Pierre works at a farm four kilometres from here and he will take you there tomorrow. Soon you will go with him into the town and he will show you the hotel where you are going to stay the night. You have some money?'

'Yes, plenty, thank you.'

'Tomorrow at 11.30 a.m. he will meet you outside your hotel and will then take you to a house where there are two bicycles. You will cycle together to the farm.'

It was superb news. I looked at Pierre with intense appreciation and shook his hand. My hostess patted him on the shoulder.

'You are lucky to have him, he will see you through.'

Pierre had some jobs to do. I collected my haversack from the front garden and joined the three old people in the back room and attempted to pump them for information about getting to Toulouse.

'When you get over the line you make for Châteauroux, either by bus or train. You used to be able to get a train from there to Toulouse but what happens now I don't know. Pierre will tell you.'

Pierre appeared at the garden window and tapped to indicate that he was ready. Slowly I got up and shook all three by the hand, attempting to impress on them how deep was my appreciation. It was a touching moment and the elder sister said, 'You will be all right with Pierre,' and I took her arm to the closed front door. It was opened and Pierre and I walked to the centre of the town. Men in uniform, German control and French gendarmes became a common sight.

Pierre brought me to a hotel and said,

'This is it. I will meet you here at 11.15 – not 11.30 as you were told – tomorrow and we will walk to the house for the bicycles.'

He turned and went off and I, with some trepidation, entered the hotel. It was revealing to find the bar packed with Germans some drinking and others playing various table games. I went to the desk and awaited my turn.

'Have you a single room for one night?'

'Yes, sir, will you be taking dinner?'

'No, thank you.'

I filled in the form with my identification card open on the desk.

The relief of getting a key and shutting the door of my room was considerable. There was nothing to do but sleep and the idea of doing it in a bed had a very desirable effect. There were about sixteen hours to pass and so ample time to wake, eat the contents of Madame Mayard's parcel and fall to sleep again. It was consoling not to be staying in someone's house but in a hotel where the risk was entirely personal.

My sleep was shattered by a firm banging on the door. It was past ten o'clock and doubtless someone wanted to do my room.

I shouted '*ça va*' to let the person know that I was awake and hoped that it would satisfy the maid or who ever it was. It did, which was reassuring that it was no one more sinister.

Pierre was on time and we walked together to a house with a door into a yard. Here he produced two well used bikes from a shed and leaning on his proceeded to give me some details of the next move.

The plan was to ride out of town for about five kilometres to a farm where he did part-time work. The bikes would be left in a shed and when he was satisfied that the German patrol was having lunch in a barn of the neighbouring farm we would walk down a path behind a hedge which crossed the Demarcation Line into another farm on the opposite side of the small valley.

We set off and it was interesting to see this little town, obsessed with the importance of guarding the line. There were uniforms everywhere.

Pierre imparted quite naturally a feeling of confidence. Being on a bicycle, under his guidance, making rapid progress towards the next goal gave a wonderful sense of purpose. As we got towards his farm he was looking out for the patrol. He spotted them and pointed to some woods quite a distance from the road. There were three guards crossing a cutting.

At Pierre's farm we dumped the bikes and he went off, presumably to reconnoitre. After what seemed a long time he returned.

'We are off,' he said.

I followed him through a gate of the yard down a footpath alongside a hedge, glancing nervously through the gaps at a group of barns a field away where Pierre had watched the guards go in. He told me that that was where they had lunch. There was no sign of activity or of any of them keeping a look out. One hoped the meal was sufficiently attractive to keep them off the job and to eliminate curiosity.

It was an exciting quarter of an hour's walk. Not until we had reached the buildings of the farm on the other side did my ears cease to be cocked for a shot or a shout. It must have been a good lunch.

There was no mistaking the welcome for us at the farm. Madame was buxom and full of joy and obviously delighted to see Pierre and to applaud me for a successful crossing. She had laid two places for lunch with the family and invited us to sit down. Very soon we were helping to empty the first bottle of wine.

She had much to ask Pierre. Cut off from all her old friends and neighbours on the other side of the line there was a lot she wanted to know about local gossip and events.

Pierre had not been over the line for many months which made him a very popular visitor and made me realise what fortune had come my way.

Pierre told the farmer that I wanted to go to Châteauroux. This seemed to be no problem. He explained to me that his house was between the two lines and that he could take me across the French line in the back of a lorry.

News of Pierre's arrival got further afield, neighbours came in and celebrations went on well into the afternoon.

The farmer touched my arm. It was a call to follow him through a back door into a large shed. There was no chance of seeing and thanking Pierre, he was still the centre of attraction. He had been magnificent and deserved far more than thanks but there was now a new guide and nothing to do but to hop at his command.

In the back of a lorry he covered me over with a lot of empty sacks behind some drums and snugged it all down.

'Five minutes and we will be over,' he said.

Off he drove slowly through the farm. There was a bump or two and then he opened out on the road. A few minutes later he stopped. There were footsteps and some talking and my ears became fixed on the catches of the tail-board or sounds of my friend getting down from his seat. They were agonising moments lying there hardly daring to breathe but the conversation became increasingly jocular. At last there was a pause, a reassuring sound of an accelerator boost and off we went into unoccupied France.

Some time later he pulled up to allow me to climb into the front seat with him. It was quite a drive to the station but a pleasant relaxed hour or so revelling in the joy of Free France.

At the station we shook hands very warmly and I gripped his arm to make him promise to tell Pierre that I would be eternally grateful for his wonderful guidance.

In the train to Châteauroux my thoughts drifted to a new angle; not on how to cross the Demarcation line but on how to get out of France. Connections and addresses were all exhausted and it was a problem of which direction to take. Gibraltar or Lisbon were the two obvious alternative targets and the idea of going to Toulouse to seek advice and possibly help appealed as the next step.

It was reassuring to find on arrival at Châteauroux that there was a through train, but not until the next morning.

The object in mind was to find the Portuguese Consulate and

this endeavour needed considerable thought. It might be in the telephone directory but if that was no help asking a policeman or anyone at random was risky, especially for that particular Consulate. The problem was still in mind when there on the station was an enquiry desk. This at once appealed as a possible answer, especially when the female sitting there greeted me with a smile. What a difference such a simple sign of welcome could make to a tense situation. Her spontaneous change of expression was greeted reciprocally.

'I would be most grateful if you could tell me where to find the Portuguese Consulate.'

She thought with her head in one direction and then in another but fairly obviously did not know.

Fortunately this gave her no satisfaction and saying 'One moment' she disappeared through a door at the back of the office.

To my joy she returned with a printed street map on which someone had put an ink cross to mark the Consulate.

She had certainly done her good deed for the day and I did my best to transfer my appreciation.

It was a long walk which gave me plenty of time to dwell over my approach to the problem. So much depended on the type of person and their attitude to a suspicious stranger.

The Consulate was a comparatively small building, easy to find and in response to a knock the door was opened by a male servant. He showed me into a room and invited me to sit down. He wanted to know the nature of my business.

'Is it possible to see the Consul?' I asked.

'The Consul is away, but –' he gave somebody's name – 'will see you.'

Some time later in came a little man with grey hair, smartly dressed in a well-fitting grey suit and well polished brown shoes. He greeted me by shaking hands, sat down and then asked where I had come from.

'Rouen,' I said. 'I have a special pass to visit my mother, who is very sick.'

He listened intently and then asked me if she was living in Toulouse.

To avoid answering this question I pulled out my identification card.

'Perhaps you would care to see this. You will notice that I am a male nurse.'

He looked at it carefully.

'Why have you come to see me?'

His expression was encouraging and sincere and he gave the impression of wanting to help.

There was a pause. The cogs of decision turning rapidly and hesitatingly in my cranium must almost have been audible.

'I am really an escaped prisoner of war from a German camp,' and I laid my British cards and prisoner of war metal disc on the table.

His expression remained unchanged but he pulled up his chair and studied the objects with interest. He looked me in the eye and said, 'There is nothing that I can do. This Consulate is very carefully watched and there is no way that I know of getting into Portugal. Walking the Pyrenees is very precarious and hazardous and you would almost certainly be picked up by frontier guards or mountain patrols. The best advice to give you is to go to Marseille. There is still an American Consul there. You can get a direct train from here.'

He pulled out a bit of paper and wrote down the address and handed it to me.

'Can you read that?'

'Yes.'

'Please memorise it, don't forget because it is difficult to find.'

He took the paper back and put it on his desk.

'I wish you luck,' he said.

Before leaving he asked me to repeat the address.

'Go as soon as you can because he will not be there much longer.'

CHAPTER EIGHT
Marseille

Nom de Guerre Henri Boseaux had slept or feigned sleep much of the way to Marseille and had been undisturbed by any control. The identity card bearing this name and my photo was carefully tucked into the inside pocket over the left breast from where it could be produced with ease at a moment's notice with a minimum of disturbance in a crowded compartment.

Saturday afternoon was not the best time of the week to be arriving, possibly the worst. It was unlikely that any contact could be made or any glimmer of help be forthcoming before Monday morning. During the wakeful hours on the train from Toulouse my thoughts had turned this possibility over and over. Only during waves of optimism did it seem possible that an American consul or his staff could still be around. It was over three months since Pearl Harbour and it was, to say the least, a far flung hope to imagine that they had not left long since, but the Portuguese official was very insistent that this action was worthwhile.

Leaving the station my thinking clicked back to the present and at that moment it seemed desirable to get off the streets and to find a hotel while it was still light. There was the inevitable cluster of hotels around the station area and a walk about soon settled the decision without difficulty. The place of choice was settled more by instinct than reason. It was an unpretentious second rate affair, seeming to be innocent of efficiency, spit and polish and bustle; a haven where life might move more slowly and where the slightly odd, eccentric or lonely visitor would be less conspicuous and less likely to get involved in conversation. Most of the hotels within easy reach of the station gave much the same impression.

This one had five or six rather worn stone steps up to an open front door beside which stood a large jardinière with a few welcoming daffodils. The lace curtain in the adjoining window had become detached at one corner and in released freedom displayed a shade rather less than white. Mounting the steps I entered the hall and there, seated at a little square reception desk, was an oldish lady. She had heard me coming up the steps and was watching the door; our eyes met.

'*Bon soir, Madame*,' I said in a quiet reassuring tone and touched my beret as an amiable gesture, in an attempt to allay the impact of my accent.

She was a lady, probably in her sixties, with a mound of carefully arranged greying hair, a wrinkled and drawn face, with rather prominent eyes.

'*Monsieur*,' she replied in a weak but affable way. She sat there with her hands between her thighs awaiting my request. The linoleum beneath her feet was worn.

'Have you a single room for two nights, not the most expensive?'

'Let me look,' and she reached for a book on a shelf at her side. She ran her right index finger down one page and another.

'Yes, there is a single room on the third floor.'

'Thank you.'

She wrote something down and then handed me a form.

'You have to complete that and then I will give you a key.'

It was no problem. I now knew all the answers.

'Will you be taking dinner?'

That was the dreaded question. I longed to say, 'Yes, three times each night,' but my tongue stuck to my mouth and the reply was:

'No, thank you, I shall be eating with friends this evening and tomorrow.'

She looked disappointed, shrugged her shoulders and murmured, '*Voilà*.'

'I have come from the north where food is very short and have left my ration book with my family. Would it be possible to have breakfast tomorrow without any tickets?'

'*Monsieur*, it is very difficult. Why have you not brought your ration book?'

'My family in Rouen is very short of food.'

'*C'est terrible, la guerre*.'

During the last part of the conversation I was looking her straight in the eye and without difficulty put on a glimmer of pathos.

'Here is your key. You will find the room at the back of the hotel on the third floor. You turn right at the top of the stairs.'

'Thank you very much.'

It was a relief to get there, to close the door and to know that here was a base of my own for the next two days.

By nine o'clock I had spent an enlightening evening and consumed no more than a moderation of drink. It was time to return to the hotel.

The front door was still unlocked and the hall, lit by a little oil lamp, was empty, much to my joy, because there was nothing now between me, a bedroom of my own and a bed for the night. A feeling of euphoria and overwhelming contentment enshrouded me as I let myself into the little room, got undressed and slithered down beneath the duvet.

It must have been some twelve hours or so later when I was half brought to my senses by a knock on the door. The muffled response was apparently accepted as a call to enter by the person outside. Suddenly I was fully awake. The door was being pushed open slowly and hesitatingly by a tray held by the lady of the hall, my friend of yesterday afternoon. She advanced and put it down on the foot of the bed and then stood back and smiled. It was an unbelievable sight and before I could think of a suitable tribute, she said,

'*Voilà – c'est pour vous*.'

'How marvellous! You are very kind. I never expected anything like that. Thank you very much.'

With a smile broadening across her pale face she retreated backwards and disappeared through the door. On the tray were three slices of bread, some jam and a bowl of *café au lait*.

Breakfast in bed – it was out of this world. To achieve this combination meant getting a breakfast and finding a bed simultaneously and both had been comparative rarities during the last week. To have it brought by someone else made it a prize among collectors' pieces. The next quarter of an hour was sheer joy.

The Portuguese official had given me the address of the Consul but I was not sure whether it was his house, his office or a combination of the two. It was important not only to locate it but to go there and watch it, particularly on Monday morning. It was possible that there would be a policeman in uniform or a guard or warden of some sort in civilian clothes. If so, it was equally important to note if he was asking questions or demanding papers from would-be entrants.

With a sketch of the streets which I had drawn from a map in a large hotel there was no difficulty in finding the place. It was a gaunt-looking building lacking in architectural attraction and as far as could be remembered there was a high wall on to the street on either side. There were some steps up to the front door which showed no evidence of life. No lights were visible within and it seemed obviously shut up for the day or, and that was a depressing thought, permanently closed. Now seemed the best opportunity to reconnoitre the local streets and decide on a plan for the morning. There was a café quite close; it was closed at the moment but it might be a good site as an observation post from which to watch who walked in and out and with what ease this could be achieved. It would be useful as a pied à terre for waiting even if the entrance to the Consulate could not be seen from there. An hour or so was spent exploring the neighbouring streets and then I decided to return to the centre and spend an evening in the cinema, the ideal place to waste time in comparative safety and comfort. Memories of that afternoon in Rouen, some four weeks ago, came vividly to mind.

At about nine in the evening I returned to my hotel and found Madame seated at her little desk. I greeted her and sat down before climbing the stairs to the third floor and quickly prepared an imaginative account of my day.

'I found my mother. She is very ill and will probably not live long so I am pleased that I came. She is being nursed in a friend's house where there are two daughters to help.'

'What time will you be leaving tomorrow?'

'About nine o'clock, but I shall return when I have seen how my mother is.'

'Will you be staying tomorrow night?'

'May I tell you when I return after seeing my mother?'

'Yes,' was her reply, which was a great help.

The next morning there was a similar knock on my door, with the same interrupted entrance of a tray pushing open the door, followed by my good friend with the inevitable smile of the benevolent.

'*Voilà, monsieur*,' she said, as she slid it on to the foot of the bed.

'*C'est magnifique, merci beaucoup*.'

She retreated backwards, gently step by step, until she disappeared through the door. It was exactly the same breakfast and enjoyed to the full in the same leisurely way. It was a good preparation for a morning of the unknown which could easily be a complete blank and throw me back to less than square one.

I walked the route that was now familiar and within twenty

minutes was in the vicinity. A quick glance turning into the road was sufficient. There was a man standing outside the front door at the bottom of the steps. This meant that the Consulate was open but that there might be some problem in getting in. I decided to go to the café for a period of observation. It was important to see his response to anyone going into the building.

The person on duty was in civilian clothes without any distinguishing badge or insignia of office. He mostly stood still but was inclined to walk one or two paces in either direction. He gave the impression of not being very enthusiastic about his job, he seemed to be as interested in the people on the other side of the road as those passing him. Then one person stopped and spoke to him for a few moments and then mounted the steps into the Consulate. There was no inspection of papers. Another person walked to the steps, nodded to him and went in without being stopped.

I had seen enough, my papers were ready and there was nothing more to do than brave the issue come what may. I decided to go up the road, cross higher up and then walk down towards the Consulate reading the paper which I had taken care to buy on the way. The plan was to appear to be so familiar with the position of the Consulate that there was no need to look where I was going. At the second window before the door I would stop and fold the paper, tuck it under my arm, and nodding to the watchman walk up the steps, prepared at any moment to stop and produce my papers if there was any indication that he wanted to see them.

It went according to plan. At the moment of folding my paper and putting it away I looked him straight in the eye and raised my right hand to the level of my waist as a gesture of recognition. There was no reaction at all which was most surprising and suggested that his suspicion for whatever he was watching was not roused. I continued through the door and into the hall. Here no one seemed to bother about me. There was undoubted activity and a uniformed porter and two secretaries came and went. Three people were seated on a row of chairs, resigned and apprehensive. There was nothing to do but sit there and join them.

'You are going to see the Consul?' I asked.

'He is not here but I hope to see someone,' was the reply.

It soon became obvious that there was considerable activity going on. Two porters came in and out several times, carrying files and stacks of papers to a room near the front door, secretaries and clerks walked quickly with tense, preoccupied expressions.

Then a little bell rang nearby and the first of our four went towards a door and we all moved up one place.

Eventually my turn came. I was beckoned to a chair by a youngish man. He was thick-set, medium in height with a purposeful, receptive expression, but he sat there looking at me and saying nothing, obviously waiting to know the reason for my visit.

'Are you the Consul?'

'No, he has gone some time ago,' he replied in an obvious North American accent and then said, 'You are British? Were you not stopped by the French control at the door?'

'No, he said nothing.'

'You were lucky to get in.'

This seemed to be the moment to speak.

'I am an escaped prisoner of war, a British officer,' and I placed on his desk my British and International Red Cross papers and my prisoner of war metal disc.

He accepted them after a perfunctory look and said,

'There is nothing that I can do. We are leaving the country and this Consulate is closing today. We should have left last week.'

There was silence as I sat there with no inclination at all to move.

'What can I do to get across the Pyrenees?'

'I don't know,' he said. 'What sort of officer are you – artillery, infantry?' It was obvious that he had taken nothing in from the cards I put on his table.

'I am a surgeon – The Royal Army Medical Corps.'

'You have been in Germany?'

'Yes, I was captured in Dunkirk and went into Germany five months later.'

Again he said, 'There is nothing I can do – we are leaving today. You might find someone in the cafés who could help you but be very careful because Marseille is full of Germans and Italians in plain clothes and of course the French police are liable to arrest you.'

He pushed my disc and papers back to me as a final gesture.

'I called at the Portuguese Consulate in Toulouse and it was suggested that this was the place to try and so I have come all this way from the Pyrenees.'

He went into thought and got up and walked around the room.

'I'll tell you something in very strict confidence. No one is to know that any help you got in this direction came from here.'

He could have had me kissing the Bible, crossing my heart, so hungry was I for a crumb from the table. He had made up his mind to go ahead and needed no reassurance.

Out of the top drawer of his desk he produced a street map of the locality and drew a ring with his finger around the area and named a particular church as a centre from which to base my search.

'Somewhere in that area you will find an old man who sharpens knives, scissors, axes, etc. He has a trolley for his work-bench and instruments and pushes it round the district. His name is Charles and when you find him, get talking and ask for Marcelle. If you can find her she may help you. You can mention me as Josef – no more.'

With that he got up, shook me by the hand and wished me luck. He was already thinking of the next job and by the time I repeated the names he had mentioned he was almost through the door.

'Thanks a lot' seemed an appropriate response and it was doubtful that he even heard it.

Three names were indelibly fixed in my mind and the area of streets was the next obvious destination.

I left the building with a great feeling of relief; there was hope and something to chase. A plan while escaping was equivalent to a weapon when fighting, an essential without which it was a pointless waste of intention. Now walking was a pleasure and one street slipped past another and as the area came near I could spot the church that he had described by the shape of its tower. Each street was now of intense interest, anything parked was for inspection but there was nothing resembling a grinder's barrow.

Round the church area I went in increasing orbits and then suddenly, when my hopes were beginning to sag, I spotted something very suspicious. It was a barrow parked the other side of a van, but it was not possible to see if there was anyone there until clear of the large bulk of the van. Sure enough, as I got clear, there was an old man standing on the pavement side of the barrow, sharpening something on a stone which he was turning with a foot pedal. With relaxed ease and rhythm he pedalled away, applying his attention at that moment to a carving knife. He showed no sign of loss of concentration when a passer-by stopped to watch. It was just part of his trade and accepted as a natural phenomenon that others should be attracted by an artist at work. He had on a khaki woollen hat and an old mackintosh over an overcoat. A little grey beard projected above his collar and on his hands were black mittens.

The pedalling stopped and he examined carefully the edge of the knife by running his thumb and finger up and down the blade. Satisfied, he placed it in a box to his right and selected another from a box on the left. Away went the pedal again and the next blade was on its way. There had been no glance away from his work and no invitation to interrupt. I decided to move and stand near the box on his right so that possibly after the next he could be persuaded to break off for a little.

Next time he did glance up. Little dark, penetrating eyes under thick greying eyebrows fixed me for one moment.

'That will make someone very pleased.' I said the first thing that came to my head so as to get something off at the right moment.

'Why?'

'A job well done generally does please people.'

'*Ou, la, la*,' he replied and seemed to be happy to have an excuse to take a moment off.

'You have been doing this for very many years?'

'Since the war,' he said. 'It's about twenty-three years since I started, here in Marseille.'

'Then I have been watching the real artist,' and this seemed to please him. So far so good.

'I am looking for someone and when I saw you it occurred to me immediately that you would know the district and the people who live here as well as anyone.'

He looked up, this time with vigilance and expectancy, but said nothing. As he turned away he started to pick up another knife and then in an apparently offhand manner he said:

'Who are you looking for?'

'Marcelle.'

'Marcelle who?' he replied.

'I know no other name. The person who sent me here told me to mention Josef and to ask you for the address of Marcelle.'

He knew. The bell had rung and there was silence while he thought.

He turned round and pointed past the van to the road I had come from.

'You go back to that road, turn right and walk for half a kilometre. Then on the right you will see a road named . . . . This is your road. Memorise it but do not write it or the number down.' He asked me to repeat the name of the road.

'The number is 23.'

From that moment the conversation had finished. The next knife had been selected and the pedal once more was in action. The screech of the grindstone almost drowned my grateful response because that was the way he wished it.

So it seemed that there really was a Marcelle. There was sufficient reassurance to boost my power of imagination during a walk which asked for nothing less than that.

The road curved slightly to the left and on both sides were terraced houses. There was no difficulty in finding 23, so suddenly there it was. The windows were all lined with muslin. There were three storeys of them and no sign of any life. The door was unpretentious, a small window in its upper third through which no light could be seen.

I pressed the bell and could hear it ring inside and stood there alert with hope. There was no response. I pressed again, there was still no result, no footsteps, no lights being switched on, no head at an overhead window, just nothing. The place was dead. One more try on the bell confirmed the inevitable conclusion. That door, a moment ago glittering in a golden hue of expectancy, had become a damp squib.

My mind went back to Rouen, a little old lady in a shawl with grey hairs blowing over her forehead. '*Rien à faire, monsieur,*' she had said. But why should she be in, why not shopping, visiting friends? There was no reason to be unduly depressed. It was more likely than not that she would be out at this time of day. I decided to return in two hours and meanwhile would waste the time in the middle of town with the cafés and shops in preference to wandering round the quiet roads of that less busy part of the city.

Soon after one o'clock I was back at the same door with renewed hope but a fundamental conviction that nothing would happen. I rang the bell and waited. There were no steps, not a sound. Then just as I was going to press again the door opened and there stood a young lady expectantly looking me in the eye.

'*Marcelle*?'

'*Oui – comment*?'

This was a very natural reply and it called for a clear explanation. She was confronted by a complete stranger without warning of such a visit.

'I was this morning talking to Charles, an old man who sharpens knives and has a barrow near here. He said that you were a good friend of his and gave me your address.'

'How do you know Charles?'

'From Josef.'

Marcelle's expression changed from apprehension to one of interest.

'When did you see Josef?'

'This morning, in his office.'

Marcelle beckoned me to come in and closed the door. She led the way down a passage to a small sitting room and invited me to sit down beside her on a sofa with a slight curve at each end so that we finished up almost facing each other. Marcelle was dressed in a pink blouse and black skirt. She was medium in height and buxom but she sat with an ease and buoyancy that graced the rather antiquated piece of furniture that gave us support.

'So you saw Josef this morning. I thought he had left the country.'

'He is going today. At first he said that there was nothing he could do and then after considerable thought, suggested that I make contact with you.'

'You must tell me who you are.'

'I am a British officer, a doctor, escaped from a German prisoner-of-war camp. Here is my identity card and my International Red Cross card.'

While she examined them my hand reached down inside my shirt for the metal disc.

'This is my *Kriegsgefangener* disc.'

Her hand went out for that and she turned it over and examined it with obvious interest. This was followed by my French card of identity.

'I was hidden in Rouen by some de Gaullists and they got these papers. That is my present name and I am a male nurse visiting my sick mother.'

'So you are a French nurse and a British doctor.' Marcelle's face broke into an attractive smile with a symmetrical dimple. She had been listening with intent to me spilling the beans without reserve. Her expression was one of receptive interest and encouragement conducive to confidence and perhaps saying too much.

'What are your plans now?'

'I want to get into Spain but when I was in Toulouse, instead of going south the Portuguese Consulate advised me to come to Marseille.'

'How will you get into Spain?'

'I have no plan but intend getting near to the border by train and then walking over the mountains.'

'You know where to go?' she asked.

'No, I have never been here before and have no plans or instructions.'

'It is very difficult and you will almost certainly be picked up in the mountains by the border patrols.'

There was a pause because there seemed very little else to say.

'Perhaps it would have been better to try from Toulouse. The mountains are much nearer there; in which case coming to Marseille was a mistake,' I added.

'Crossing the Pyrenees anywhere is difficult if you have no local knowledge and there is still a lot of snow at this time of year.'

'What can I do?'

There was another pause and then Marcelle moved nearer to me on the sofa and said:

'Do you know Mario?'

'No.'

'You must meet him. He will be here in Marseille in a few days and he may be able to help you. You can stay here until he comes, when I will put you in contact with him.'

'I can stay here?'

'Yes.'

Excitedly I said, 'I have some money but no ration cards' and watched Marcelle's face. Her expression radiated nothing but affirmative confidence. There seemed no immediate difficulty to my staying there.

'Have you any baggage?'

'Yes, at the hotel near the station which has been my home for two nights. There is no difficulty in getting that.'

'You know your way?'

'From the Canebière but how would you get there from here?'

Marcelle gave me a simple description of how to get to the Canebière. It was a walk of about fifteen minutes.

'You will be back then in about an hour?'

'Yes, will you be in?'

'Certainly,' she replied without any hesitation and at that point I made an effort to stand up and stretch my legs.

How easy it had suddenly become. It seemed almost her job to welcome and accommodate strange men but I should see. Either I was on to something good or I was putting my head into a well greased noose. All my cards were on the table and if she wanted to – it was just not worth thinking about. Walking back to the hotel with Marcelle in mind was sheer joy; life had certainly taken on a happy turn.

Who was Mario? What could he do to help and where did he come from? How could she feed me without ration cards? There was certainly insufficient money left to buy much on the black market. Such questions gave ample food for thought during the search for the way back to the hotel, but my steps were buoyant and purposeful and climbing the stairs to the third floor of the hotel was child's play compared to the evening before.

Madame was not in the hall but she soon appeared.

'Will you be staying tonight?'

'No', I said, 'my mother is no better but I don't think I shall stay any longer.'

Madame sat down at her little desk and after some thought wrote in a few figures which could be nothing other than my bill. She added it up again and passed it over with a degree of askance in her upward glance but it was obvious, before looking at it, that it would be lenient, and so it was.

'You have a very content and grateful customer. Thank you a thousand times.'

'*Au revoir, Monsieur*,' she said, and a smile spread across her face as much as to say 'it is my pleasure and good luck.' Doubtless she had guessed my country of origin before she brought up the first breakfast.

Marcelle's house was run in a very definite and purposeful way which was not immediately apparent. But the longer one stayed there the more obvious it became that it ticked in a dynamic pattern and that her heart was in her job. There was also little doubt that she had a great affinity for the opposite sex and that the feeling was mutual. To have men in her house and to cater for their basic comforts and needs was her natural vocation and indeed a very valuable and fulfilling war effort. With great energy, initiative and verve she bustled about the house, coping with anyone that came. She was the chef, the hostess, the only person who knew what each of us was. She was the go-between, a job that she did splendidly well, making us all sense a touch of home. There were three, sometimes four, lodgers who worked away all day and came there for a meal and a bed. Communication between them was difficult. There was a language problem and a secretive element in that they had no wish to probe into each other's business. One was a German who, Marcelle had let slip, had left the army in Russia. One was a Pole and the other two were of unknown origin. None spoke more than a few words of English.

Marcelle had the gift of producing meals from very little. There was always a plate of hot soup and bread followed by something hot and bulky with a taste of artistry from her cupboard. It was made up of various vegetables and a smattering of meat in unrecognisable small pieces. How she produced this daily meal was a mystery but she never complained or spoke of the problems she had in shopping. Ration cards and money were welcome but not essential. I had no ration card and when she knew the amount of money in my pocket she refused to take any.

Without a job I remained in the house most of the day, the more permanent lodger, waiting, she explained, to see Mario. The explanation never went further than that, no suggestion as to who he was, where he came from or for what purpose, but Marcelle told me to keep it entirely to myself and to mention his name to no one. It was not for me to probe or wonder whether Marcelle had my interests at heart; if she had not she gave a very good impression of the opposite.

It was not difficult to imagine Marseille as a plug hole of the south-west corner of Europe, where would-be evaders congregated and from where the exit tube was too small and likely to become clogged. Meanwhile there might be many of various nationalities hanging around awaiting an opportunity to get out. Meeting the characters in Marcelle's house gave me that impression and my hope was that Mario would be an aid to priority.

Marcelle had told me a little of her history. At the time of the invasion of Belgium, her husband had at an early stage taken off his uniform and come home. She had left him forthwith and driven down through France with nothing more than the dress she put on that morning. She had been in this house for over a year and become established in looking after people.

On the third day after I arrived Marcelle found me alone reading in a corner and came and sat close. In a low but excited voice she said:

'Mario is coming tomorrow. I will take you to meet him, so be ready here at ten o'clock. It is good news, I did not expect him to come so soon.'

Next morning we set off down the street and after walking about a kilometre came to a park. It was a nice sunny morning and a few had already started taking the air. We walked through the gates and down a wide path until we came to two seats sheltered from the north by a semicircle of hedge. Marcelle sat down and indicated to me to take the other.

'Mario will come here and talk to you. It is important that you answer all his questions as well as you can.'

Seated there in apprehension every single male became a potential focus of interest but none stopped or took any notice of us. Then suddenly Marcelle put her hand on my knee. 'There he is', she said. Coming round the path from the other side was a man of middle height, walking with neat dapper steps and his head held up in observation. He wore a soft black hat with the front brim turned down and carried a cane in his right hand. Marcelle pretended not to notice him, got up and walked away in the other direction as soon as she was assured that he had spotted us. Mario was dressed in a dark suit and was sartorially conspicuous among the other strollers. Without hesitation he nodded to me and came and sat in the empty chair.

'You know Marcelle?'

'Yes, she is a great girl and told me that one day you might return to Marseille.'

'You are British?'

'Yes, an officer in the Army Medical Corps. I have my military identity card, my International Red Cross card and my prisoner of war disc.'

'Marcelle has seen them. I am going to ask you some questions, the answers to which will be checked. This is the only way that you can prove to me that you are the owner of these papers and the prisoner of war disc.'

He wrote down my name, rank, unit and number and date where captured and my date of birth.

'Where did your parents live at the time of your birth?'

'At 4, Elmhurst Road, Dovercourt, Essex.'

'Where were you at school at the age of fourteen?'

'Cranleigh, Surrey.'

'Who was your history master?'

'Purvis.'

'Who is your nearest relative?'

'My father, J.H. Newman, of Mannofield, Ingatestone, Essex.'

'The name of a godmother?'

'Mrs S.P. Marriage.'

With that he closed his little book and put it away.

He told me that it would take some time to check the answers but that he would let Marcelle know when he returned. There was no wasted conversation and he got up and left and walked back to the gate where we had first spotted him. He had talked good English but had a slight accent which was not easy to designate. He had a sallow complexion but was dressed like an English gentleman. It was difficult to place his origin, maybe he was Eastern European.

He was gone after no more than ten minutes together and there was nothing left to bite on, just a hope that he would come back with some good news.

Two days later Marcelle told me that her Russian boyfriend would be coming to stay for a weekend and that I must get out. If he found me there he would kill me. She told me that in no uncertain terms. The message was clear and being dependent there was no alternative but to accept the plan, degrading and inconvenient as it was and it never became obvious whether the potential dislike had an amorous or political basis.

The old lady who called to take me away soon won my heart. She was a widow who had been married to an Englishman who lived in Marseille and had worked for Thomas Cook, the travel agents. She had obviously adored her husband and it was apparent before long that some of her undispensed attention was being transferred to me. Her face reflected the years of contentment and happiness, but her home was very humble and the amenities minimal. She lived in one room with a small kitchenette and as soon as we arrived after a long walk she made a pot of tea. She spoke English with ease and had apparently at some time worked in the agency. She told me all about her husband and the lovely holidays that they had enjoyed under the benefits of working for such a firm. She mentioned no children and her conversation was composed entirely of small talk. If she knew anything of what went on in wartime Marseille, there was no indication of such and she told me nothing of that sort.

Doubtless she had learnt a lot about diplomacy, tact and confidential information from her association with Thomas Cook. We talked while she cooked the supper. She was keen to know all about Great Britain and how it was standing up to the war, but much more interested in England before the war, where they had spent some of their holidays. She explained that she was going to cut the room into half so as to make two bedrooms. A blanket was produced and hung from hooks on either wall by brass rings sewn to the blanket. It was not the first time that it had been hung and one could imagine the various characters that this old dear had accommodated in the past. From a cupboard came a camp bed and some blankets and with tender care she made it up into a couch fit for a prince.

'You will be all right?'

'Absolutely. There will be no difficulty in getting to sleep.'

And so she slipped round to her side of the hanging blanket, content that what she was doing would have won the highest praise from her husband. MI9 would doubtless have approved, but how much she knew about that was wrapped up well below the surface.

'*Dormez bien.*'

'*Et vous aussi.*'

'*Oui, merci.*'

The night passed without incident and Sunday was a lovely day from the start. By the middle of the morning it was quite hot and my friend suggested that we go for a walk in the gardens.

She had put on a long grey, light, dress and taken great care with her hair on top of which she set a summery pink hat with a brim. She took a grey parasol which was opened as soon as we arrived in the park. From then on it was a genteel stroll through a beautiful open park with a view over the harbour.

Back in the security of her maisonette she cooked lunch and then showed me lots of pre-war photos, mostly of her husband and herself on holiday.

On the wall was a pipe rack with half a dozen pipes. After half an hour spent with the photos she presented me with one of the pipes as a crowning nostalgic gesture.

Monday afternoon saw me back in Marcelle's house, welcomed in the warmest terms; presumably my would-be assassin had gone. He was not mentioned.

Sometimes Marcelle invited me to go shopping and it was my job to carry the heavy basket mostly filled up with vegetables. One afternoon we went to a cinema but apart from these little excursions the days and nights slipped by in anticipation of the future. Mario had impressed me as an important contact and his interrogation as a higher examination in the field of evasion. When would he return was continually on my mind but even more engaging was his wish to see me again. To fail the test was curtains and he would make no further contact.

I had been with Marcelle nearly three weeks, getting more and more convinced that he would not see me again when one morning early Marcelle slipped into my room and sitting on my bed said,

'He is going to see you – this morning.'

I woke up very quickly, listened to the great news and hugged her until she pushed me away.

'You have to be there, at the same place, at ten a.m. It is good news.'

'How good?' I said, hoping even then that she would tell me something more, but she stuck to the minimum but added:

'You will have to take your things with you because you will not come back here.'

That told me a great deal. There was very little in my case, the old scraps of food had now been abandoned except for the lumps of sugar which were maintained as an absolute reserve; some underwear and a light mackintosh and a very worn cardigan. As she left me she put her index finger to her mouth.

'Say nothing to anyone', she whispered, 'just slip out.'

I tried to pull her back on to the bed to show her in a physical way what she deserved but she was too quick in the draw and was out of the door before my feet were on the floor.

When the time came to go Marcelle was nowhere to be found, she had gone shopping; so typical of her. Demonstrations of gratitude were not her métier. She preferred to go her own way and choose the choosing.

Waiting in the park brought back memories of attending to hear the results of examinations in my student days. But this was worse. Ten o'clock had been the suggested time but by eleven there was no sign of Mario. Then lo and behold, a few minutes later, there he was, his dapper gait, cane and black soft hat unmistakable.

He came up and stood behind my chair.

'You must follow me twenty yards behind. If I stop you must divert and follow me when I move off again. Have nothing whatever to do with me, just follow and when I go into a tall building on the edge of the port follow me in.'

Mario moved off, walking in his characteristic way, and I kept a distance the length of a cricket pitch behind him. Before long we came to the old port and went along the east side. Halfway down I noticed Mario slip into a tall block of flats.

He climbed the stairs and I followed to the fifth floor. Here he selected a door and carefully pressed the button three times. Within a few moments it was opened by a lady in Red Cross uniform.

She smiled warmly at Mario and beckoned us in. Little did I

know then that this was the threshold to the best escape and evasion line of Marseille and the Eastern Pyrenees. It was the Pat line and our hostess was Madame Nouveau.

CHAPTER NINE
The Pat Line

Renée Nouveau was slight and dark and looked immaculate in her uniform with a red cross on her breast. She greeted Mario with warmth and he bent over and kissed her hand before turning round to introduce me as Philip. She welcomed me to her home and hoped that it would be a help on my way. As we shook hands I thanked her profoundly for taking me in.

She took me around the flat and showed me my room where there was a very comfortable looking bed, a shelf of English books and a little pile of clean underclothes. Then she turned to me and said,

'We have to be very careful here about noise. It is important that the neighbours in the flat below do not know that we have lodgers so you must always wear carpet slippers and walk about with gentle steps. Also please keep away from the windows so that you cannot be seen from above or below. If you are left alone in the flat open the door only for three knocks or rings, otherwise ignore it.' Then, as an afterthought, with a glint in her eye, she added, 'You will be allowed four cigarettes a day.'

It was impossible to believe that life had changed to such controlled efficiency and apparent security and that the eternal idea of what to do next had been taken over by someone else.

'I am sure you would like a bath and a change into clean clothes.'

Meanwhile a pot of coffee had been placed on a table and Renée invited Mario and myself to join her. She was obviously keen to know more about this new stranger in her flat and she listened with great care to everything Mario had to say. They both knew full well that it was the easiest thing in the world to swallow an unpleasant customer and she and her husband had to rely entirely on Mario as a diagnostic filter. He did this to her satisfaction and I added a few anecdotes to support the impression. Her expression was entirely sincere and her eyes radiated an intense and enthusiastic reassurance that all was in control.

She turned to me and said:

'There is nothing for you to do here except to wait until the next move is planned. My husband will be here tomorrow and he may be able to give you further news. I hope you will have breakfast with him in the library.'

'I know very little of what goes on but I am convinced that luck has come my way, thanks to you and Mario. Sitting quietly and reading is no problem, I can do that for days.'

'There are some English books in your room and the maid will get you some food because I spend most of my time in hospital. We have many old war wounds and accident cases which you will know all about because Mario tells me you are a surgeon.'

This flat, situated on the fifth floor of a modern block, was on the Quai de Rive-Neuve, the east side of the old port. It commanded a superb view over the Port and the sea beyond. Through a large bay window wafted the smell of the sea and all that goes with a busy fishing port. I stood there and marvelled at the magnificent sight, keeping a little back from the window as she had warned me, but revelling in the sense of purpose and progress which now allowed Marseille to be looked on as a place of passage and not of bewilderment where the frustration of waiting mounted daily.

By 7.30 a.m. I was dressed and sitting in the big room awaiting further instructions. Before long Renée appeared, already clad in her Red Cross uniform, and greeted me with a reassuring smile, indicating that I should follow her.

At the other end of the room she led the way through a door which let us into another large room with rows of book shelves from floor to ceiling.

'Louis will be with you in a few moments,' she said and withdrew.

Space had been found between the bookshelves to set a small table with a chair at each end. It was laid for a meal.

As Renée had forecast, within a minute or so the door opened swiftly and in came a man who made straight for my right hand and looking me in the eye said, 'Philip Newman I believe. I am Louis Nouveau and delighted to meet you.'

'It is marvellous to be here and I am most grateful,' I replied.

His appearance was quite unforgettable. Thin, of medium height, wearing a light grey, well tailored suit with a spotted bow tie, his attitude at once suggested activity and competence. He had a small moustache and wore horn-rimmed glasses and his greying hair was slightly deranged. His expression of sincerity broke very quickly into one of humour and gaiety.

'I like to eat breakfast among my books, it gives me food for thought for a busy day.' He beckoned me to one of the chairs.

'Mario has told me some things about you and I want to ask you a few more details. He told me that you are English and I am now convinced that he is correct,' and with a laugh added, 'You really couldn't be anything else.'

I smiled and at first made no reply but was thinking the same way. Louis could be nothing but a Frenchman, but he spoke immaculate English whereas my French was a halting mixture of school grammar and *poilu* and Rouen vernacular.

'You must be right. I was told the same thing in Rouen by the person who picked me up on the street.'

While he was talking and I was guzzling fish he got up and reached for a large book, the first of a series of volumes on one of the shelves. He brought it down to the table. It was Volume I, *Oeuvres Completes de Voltaire*. Carefully he turned the pages over until finding some special place. He asked me my name, unit, where captured and from where escaped, my home address and nearest relative. All this he wrote very carefully and minutely along the inner part of the page parallel with the binding and when finished he pushed it over to show me.

'You are the sixty-fifth person through this file,' he said, with obvious pride, and I noted that it corresponded to the number of the page.

'Some of our visitors have stayed here two or three weeks either awaiting the next move or because they were wounded or not well,' he added. 'You know now why you wear special sneakers,' and laughingly glanced down under the tablecloth to see my feet cluttered with very hairy slippers.

'That should prevent you getting cold feet,' he quipped, and still laughing looked me in the face. Then his expression changed and he said nothing for a while. It seemed a good moment to say something in appreciation for his hospitality and the great risk that he and his wife accepted as a normal duty.

'I know very little of what goes on but I am convinced of my good fortune to be here and of my gratitude to you and others who have made it possible.'

He made no response and continued deep in thought, accepting my appreciation as a cat would a gentle stroke along the centre of its back. By his next remark it was apparent that he had been weighing up the future, the plans for the next move and how much to tell me.

He looked at me and said, 'At present there is no definite date but soon you will move to Toulouse where there is a point of rendezvous for the next party to cross the Pyrenees. When this party is complete you will go by train to the Spanish border. Then comes a strenuous walk up and over the mountains which takes two nights and a day. You need to be fit, carrying as little as possible because the guide goes at a good pace and is very disinclined to stop for anyone who cannot keep up. The guides are young and able and used to that sort of walking where the snow may be deep and the paths difficult to find.'

He noticed an apprehensive look on my face and said,

'You can spend your time here doing leg exercises and knees bend and straightening but in carpet slippers please,' and he laughed.

He picked up the volume of Voltaire and was about to return it to the shelf when it suddenly occurred to me to ask him about someone else who had got out of Sotteville in Rouen.

'Did a Bob Challenor come here by any chance?'

Louis' eyes lit up. 'Yes, of course. He was here about a month ago; a little man with a patch over one eye, a very amusing character.' He set the volume down again and turned the pages.

'Yes, here he is on Page 55. Major Challenor, escaped February 1942 from Herlag near Rouen, taken prisoner 1st June at Nolleval. I can remember him very well but have no further news of him. Presumably he must by now have got home or at least to Gibraltar. If anything had gone wrong I should have heard.'

Volume I was returned to its shelf, its secret mine of information camouflaged among the other sixty-nine.

Louis turned to me and said,

'Can I see your papers, just to check that all is in order?'

These needed fetching from my room. I set them down on the table. Louis looked at them carefully and seemed to approve.

'That's all right,' he said, 'and now I must be off. Remember to open the front door for three knocks or rings only. I don't know when I shall be back but next time we meet you may be on your way. Good luck with the exercises. *Au revoir*.'

And so Louis left me to finish my breakfast in the library of two thousand books. In a few minutes the door opened and in came Renée. She sat at the table to tell me that she was going to the hospital but would be back for lunch. During the morning the cook would come to prepare the meal. She had her own key and would let herself in without ringing the bell.

'You will be pleased to hear that Louis is perfectly happy. It was such a reassurance that you mentioned Bob Challenor. I know that you had a good pasting from Mario and he does his job thoroughly but we have to be very careful who we accept and pass on especially when they are alone. With couples or more who are friends it is much easier. It may have seemed to you that the papers you carried were sufficient proof of your identity but they mean very little. An impostor would almost certainly carry papers to verify his identity and speak good English. Sometimes characters arrive here, having been given this address, with nothing but papers to support their request for help and they are very difficult to deal with. Bob was here a few days and we enjoyed his company and I hope he is now in England.'

'What luck I happened to remember him and that Louis's file showed that he escaped from the same camp in Rouen.'

Renée got to her feet and said,

'I must be on my way, I hope you can amuse yourself.'

She left me thinking hard and full of admiration for the dangerous job that she and Louis did together, a supreme war effort. To them we were known as parcels, parcels which had to be carefully examined, rejected or accepted and stamped and passed on down the line. They were parcels that might contain a bomb and go off at any time. Fortunately it was now accepted that this particular parcel had no bomb inside and was fair game to proceed forward.

It was obvious, after what Louis had said, that preparation for the journey was one essential that could be coped with in the period of waiting for the next move. I decided on an intensive course of physical exercise to strengthen my leg muscles for the mountains. Going back into the main room I selected a wooden chair with protruding arms and grasping these it was easy to do a full knees bend, sit on my heels and then stand up straight. This was it, to be repeated and repeated until exhausted, followed by a rest and then repeated again and again until my legs could take no more.

This I was doing when the door opened without a knock and in came a lady, presumed to be the cook.

'*Bonjour, Monsieur*,' she said without surprise.

'You knew that I was here?'

'Oh, yes, Madame told me this morning when she brought some meat, she had been shopping for lunch.'

'Do not be surprised when you see me dancing up and down like a yo-yo.'

'Yo-yo – what is it?'

'A circle of wood that winds up and down on a piece of string, like this' and I moved my hand up and down to give her the idea.

'But I go up and down on my legs to strengthen my muscles for climbing the mountains, so!'

This was followed by a demonstration. She burst into laughter and slapped her thigh.

'Three hundred times an hour,' I added.

By midday both my legs were aching violently and were sore and it seemed had had enough for a time, but it was a start and a sense of achievement began to infiltrate the static frustration.

I was studying the map of the country north of the Pyrenees, in particular the railway down to the Spanish border, when the door opened again, without a knock, and in came Renée.

She made straight for the kitchen and there doubtless was an exchange of events since their last encounter. It was too far away to catch the gist of conversation but it was voluble and animated. Then Renée came into the big room and said,

'Philip, I have good news for you. You are going tomorrow. This is very quick. I saw Louis about an hour ago and he had just heard. So you will have to be up very early in the morning.'

'Where shall I go?' I asked.

'Perhaps to Toulouse. I am not certain but Louis will be in tonight and tell you what to do and when you leave.'

'Louis has told me to get fit and I have started doing exercises this morning. Can I leave the flat and go for a long walk this afternoon?'

She was silent for a moment.

'Yes, if you tell me about what time you will return and give the usual three knocks.'

I suggested 4.30 p.m. and she agreed.

This would give me three hours, leaving immediately after lunch.

'The best way would be to go up one of the streets at the back of us and walk to the Notre Dame de la Garde, a big church on top of the hill and then go straight on down to the promenade and continue as far as you like along the coast road. That will get some fresh air into your lungs,' she added after taking a deep breath and stretching her arms sideways above her head. Then as an afterthought she added, 'Don't pick up any girl friends or get involved in idle conversation.'

'I shall have to keep my desires on ice.'

'Exactly,' she added, with a gentle smile of confirmation. 'Keep well away from the old town round the port; the coast roads and promenade are much healthier and will give you all the exercise you need for climbing mountains.'

Walking fast for three hours was exhilarating and gave a purposeful feeling of physical satisfaction which was long overdue. The door of the flat was opened almost at once by Renée who looked very relieved.

'You are back without any trouble. I was afraid you might lose your way and have to start asking for this address.'

'No, I have a very strong homing instinct and the Notre Dame de la Garde is an excellent guide. I had been all round the old port exploring my way on the first night that I arrived.'

Renée was obviously pleased to see me back before Louis arrived.

Within a few minutes there were some more knocks on the door and in came Mario Prassinos. He was as composed as usual, carrying his mahogany stick and hat, greeting Renée with sincere affection and nodding to me. It soon became obvious that he wanted to talk with Renée alone so that I withdrew to my room and started another bout of leg strengtheners as an appetiser for supper.

Louis came in late that evening, long after the three of us had eaten. He was delighted with the news of my departure and after he had had something to eat himself took me to a corner couch for a chat.

'I have your railway ticket to Toulouse and will give it to you tomorrow morning when we leave. I shall walk to the station and you must follow twenty or thirty metres behind. When I get to the station I shall go to the bookstall to buy a paper. Just stand and watch me but don't buy a paper, because the man at the bookstall is an acquaintance and it is better that he doesn't know that I have someone with me.'

Louis then paused for thought.

'Notice where I go and stand with my paper. It will be opposite and about twenty metres from the entrance to the platform for the train to Toulouse. As I wait there you should see a priest come and talk to me. He is going to Toulouse on the same train and will pick you up outside the barrier on Toulouse Station. Watch him and go on to the platform after him; by then he will have seen what you look like.'

'Will he be dressed as a priest?' I asked.

'Yes, and he is going to wear a fawn raincoat over his black suit. His collar will be visible.'

Then there was a pause.

'He will get on to the train and will watch you pass him and notice where you get on further up.'

'Right,' I said, and nodded my head. 'That all seems perfectly clear,' and I repeated the instructions for his approval.

'Now', said Louis, 'from the time you leave this flat you are alone until you get through the barrier on Toulouse Station. There you should be picked up by the priest and taken to your destination, but who knows things might go wrong and no priest appear. In this event you will continue alone and this is what you do.' Here he patted me on the knee and said, 'Listen very carefully, because if you slip up on this move you will be lost for good. You have to get to the Hôtel de Paris – remember, the Hôtel de Paris. It is well known and easy to find in the centre of the city. When you get there you will go through the main entrance into a glass-roofed courtyard surrounded by an inside rockery. Sitting at the kiosk will probably be a thick-set lady dressed in black with a white scarf tied over her head. She is Madame Mongelard and invariably dressed like that, all in black except for the scarf. You go up to her and say you have come to see Francis. If there is no one there you tap on the window of the kiosk. Wait until someone appears and ask for Francis, that is your password. It is Francis Blanchain who will look after you while you are in Toulouse.'

'Thank you for telling me all that. What time shall I be ready?'

'We shall leave about seven o'clock,' Louis added, 'after some breakfast.'

A few minutes later I saw Mario gathering up his things, the inevitable soft black hat and cane. He came to me to say goodbye. I clutched his arm and thanked him deeply for all he had done.

Louis appeared for breakfast dressed as before in a light grey suit and spotted bow tie. All he wanted was a cup of coffee but he insisted that it was important for me to eat something because there was no certainty about the next meal.

He got up and searched his briefcase and then turned to me.

'Here is your ticket, Philip, I hope you get home safely,' and his piercing grey eyes fixed on me with a benign smile reflecting the satisfaction of the delivery of another parcel. We were the fruits of his labours and the exacting and dangerous duties which the war effort demanded for himself and his colleagues.

'Whatever happens I shall never forget all that you and Renée have done to put me on the path for home,' I replied.

Louis had decided to go down by the stairs and to await my arrival in the lift before walking out from the block as leader. It was a sunny crisp morning with the harbour full of activity. The fish stalls were already busy with the catch that must have come in earlier that morning and as we filtered our individual ways through the different groups of activity it was important not to lose contact. Louis walked at a reasonable pace but was disinclined to turn round to check that his follower was still there.

At the top of the port, crossing to the Canebière he ran into someone he knew and stopped to talk. It lasted only a minute or so but as soon as they had parted off he went without a glance in my direction. I was learning that following was an art requiring constant vigilance. At this spot there was plenty to watch but in an isolated area sudden disconnection could need careful disguise.

Before eight o'clock Louis had bought his paper and reached the correct place near the barrier. He stood there waiting and gazing around as so many people do on a station, with a look of ever hopeful expectancy. Unfolding his paper he started to read and then sure enough someone approached and started to talk to him. It was a priest wearing a fawn raincoat. They continued deep in conversation while I watched carefully, particularly for the moment when he would turn round and have a look at me. Louis had arranged to blow his nose when quite convinced that the priest knew what his charge looked like. The moment came while Louis was talking and looking somewhere else the priest turned the other way and took me in. No action was required on my part except to watch for the concluding sign. His Reverence obviously had some discouraging remarks to make about my appearance, and then I saw Louis feel for something in his pocket; out came a handkerchief and he gave his nose a hearty blow.

There was no hurry. Conversation continued with gentle gestures and a laugh or two for a few minutes and gradually the priest showed signs of withdrawal. He looked at the station clock and then at his watch. They shook hands and he was off through the barrier with me following. He got into a carriage halfway up the train and I passed him and found a seat two carriages further up.

In the compartment were five other people; two engaged in conversation sat by the window. The others fortunately seemed occupied with their own thoughts but as usual the technique for me was to feign sleep so as to avoid conversation and to have my papers readily available in my inside left breast pocket in case I was aroused suddenly by a control or ticket inspector.

It was to be a journey of about seven hours and Louis had told me that there was no definite point of control, that with luck there would be none but at any moment one should be prepared for it.

Four hours later to my great surprise someone came into the compartment and pushed his bottom on to the seat on our side, next to me. Seeing me with my eyes closed he touched my hands, which were on my lap, and waved a paper at me.

'Would you care to read the paper?' he asked.

Looking up now with my eyes wide open, it suddenly occurred to me that it was the priest. He pushed the opened paper into my hands and momentarily pointed to the top of the first page. He sat there while his message got home. Written in pencil across the top of the front page was:

'If you would like lunch follow me.'

It was astounding but having caught his eye we were up and walking down the corridor without a thought as to the impression that it would have created on my travelling companions. To my amazement there were two reserved seats for us.

'My name is Dennis and yours Philip, I think.'

We shook hands and smiled at each other and sat down and then I burst our laughing.

'*C'est formidable, merci beaucoup*,' was the reaction which seized me at that moment. It was difficult to believe after all the detailed precautions that were taken on Marseille Station.

There were no questions to be asked about a free lunch; without ration cards and a delightful companion who was willing to do nearly all the talking about things of common interest. There was soup, some potatoes with sliced meat roll and bread and cheese to finish a meal never to be forgotten by a chronic escaper. It was sufficient to last for two or three days.

Dennis had obviously taken on more than duty demanded and it was typical apparently of his generosity to have paid for this meal and indeed run the risk of entertaining an escaped prisoner of war. He was medium in height and plumpish with more than ample dark hair and dark brown eyes and when he laughed or smiled it was an expression of genuine joy.

Time slipped by and before long Dennis warned me that we should be in Toulouse within half an hour. He suggested that we separated to pass through the barrier and rejoin outside in the station from where he would take me to the Hôtel de Paris.

The hotel was just as Louis had described. The entrance through an archway led into a large dingy hall with a glass roof and tiled floor and round the inner side of the wall was an ill attended rockery. There were some soft chairs clustered around a few tables but the seats were badly in need of upholstery attention. At a desk in a glass kiosk sat a thick-set lady dressed in black with a white scarf over her greying hair.

Dennis signalled me to one of the chairs and went forward to the lady in black. He greeted her with warmth and shook her hand and it was an obvious pleasure for her to see him. A quiet obviously confidential conversation ensued. After some minutes Dennis beckoned me to come and meet her. I was introduced as Philip and she as Madame Mongelard. He asked me for my papers. She looked at these with care and told me that she would keep them until the control had been. Dennis then chipped in.

'Don't forget your name. Here you will be known as Henri.'

Louis had told me that the password was Francis in the event of having to introduce myself and at that moment Madame Mongelard was talking about him to Dennis.

'He will be here soon so that there is no need for you to stay,' she said.

Dennis thanked her and shook her hand. He turned round and assured me that I was being left in very good hands. We walked to the front door together and then said farewell. It was a touching moment.

Two hours later a young man came in from behind her desk, looking confident and capable. Madame had much to tell him and he listened intently; finally they both looked at me and beckoned me over. As expected it was Francis and Madame told me that I was in his care and that he would now show me to my room in the hotel.

From the other end of the hall we climbed a dark, carpeted stone staircase to the third floor and then walked down a long corridor to the back of the hotel. Here Francis pushed open a door and ushered me into a room. There were two Dutchmen who got up from their chairs as soon as we came in. Francis introduced us and explained to me that they had been here two days and would tell me what to do and what not to do and where to go for food. This room, he explained, was a point of rendezvous for the party which he hoped would get off to Spain before many more days. Meanwhile we had to be prepared to lie low and cope with boredom. Francis withdrew and left me with my new friends.

We found much to talk about but it was confined to local arrangements and occurrences. We should have liked to know more about each other and how we had got there but in war time one is reticent about imparting factual knowledge without absolute certainty of the origin and motivation of the listener. From now on conversation would be with potential strangers so that there was no inclination to say very much, especially about places, lines of communication and in particular about people.

It was Helmut who suggested some food. The three of us went down a back staircase to a room near the kitchens. It was warm and had an appetising smell and before long in came a very welcome, happy looking girl with three plates of soup.

'*Voilà, bon appetit*,' she said and her hair fell over her shoulders as she lent forward. She fetched a basket of bread and three spoons and we were off. The stockpot and vegetables that followed made an ample, tasty plateful and was completed with a glass of *vin ordinaire*. As she poured out the wine Helmut introduced me to her. 'Claire, this is Henri. He has come to join us.' A beaming smile broke out for a moment but she was obviously up to her eyes in work and had no time to respond to our gesture when we raised our glasses.

Daily we left the hotel, walking round the town together or alone in different combinations. Madame Mongelard was invariably seated in her kiosk, always in black with the white scarf round her head. She said nothing but missed nothing and we were conscious that she knew how often and for how long we went out.

By the end of the week our party had swelled to six. The newcomers slept in another room but the little dining room certainly worked to capacity.

That evening Francis appeared and called us all into our room. He had a look of resolve and was anxious that we should sit down and listen.

'We go tomorrow morning early, leaving here at 6.30 a.m. You will each be given a railway ticket for your station near the Spanish border but we do not all get off at the same station.' Here Francis paired us off and told me the name of the station to look out for.

'I will give you your detailed instructions,' he added.

'At Toulouse you will all be individuals travelling alone or in pairs, which ever you wish but not all together. I will walk to the station with you and lead the way to the correct platform but shall not come on the train. During the journey do not get involved in conversation unless you speak French well, and be prepared for a control at any point. It may be a guard, a gendarme or a member of the Gestapo in civilian clothes. Have your ticket and papers easily available and if you are lucky enough to sense the approach of a control feign sleep. The most likely area of control is between Narbonne and the Spanish border especially at or just after Perpignan.'

Francis paired us off, the two Dutchmen were together and I was asked to join the most recent addition to our party. We called him Nicki.

Francis took the two of us together and told us the name of the station where we had to get off. 'It is close to the Spanish border, only a small place. You go out of the main gate into a single road where you turn left. Walk out of the village south for about half a kilometre and you will come to a single-arch stone bridge and here the road goes over a small river. There will be a man leaning over the wall of the bridge looking into the water. Brake your pace and show an interest in the stream and lean over the wall and spit into the water. That is your password and he will take you to his cottage.'

By six in the morning we were having coffee and rolls but Claire was not there. Provided as well were some extra rolls and some cheese to take with us. They were to prove very valuable.

Francis was there on the station as we found places to sit down. For me conversation was out so I decided to sit alone, to sleep or read or just to gaze out of the window. Nicki was nearby on the opposite side of the same compartment.

Nothing untoward happened until the train got to Perpignan. Here some railway officials got in and combed the train. As the train pulled into the station I made a point of leaning out of the corridor window and saw these guards get on. Returning to the compartment I touched Nicki's knee as a warning and then settled down to close my eyes. It was some time before the guards reached our coach and then we could hear each door being opened in turn.

My pulse rate was racing when the uniformed official opened our door. Automatically tickets and identity papers were produced. Most of them were passed over quite quickly but he held on to my card, looking at it carefully.

'From Rouen?' he asked.

'Yes,' I replied.

'Why have you come south?'

'To see my mother who is ill.' I had been practising saying this in my best French over and over again.

There was a horrible hesitation and then reluctantly he returned my card and closed the door.

The relief made it all worth while. No one had been allowed off the train at Perpignan until cleared by the control. As soon as it was over four of our fellow travellers left, including an old lady who needed some help with her bag.

An hour later Nicki and I got out at our little station. A few people filtered through the exit. We turned left and five minutes later, to our great joy, we spotted a little stone bridge with a man standing there. As we came closer he lent over the side and looked into the water with apparent interest.

It all happened as Francis had told us. We leaned over and spat into the water and our guide turned round and said something which I could not understand. However we followed him up the road and eventually turned down a path through a forest. The path led uphill among the trees and eventually came to a stone house. Our guide pushed open a door and ushered us into a room with people sitting on the floor. In the dim light it was possible to see the two Dutchmen but the rest were strangers. Two candles were the only source of light.

The guide made his way towards the fireplace where there was a wood fire, and leaning on the warm wall beside it said something. A voice from behind him interpreted.

'You rest now and have some food and you will leave in two hours' time.'

The remaining two of our party arrived when we were indulging ourselves in large bowls of soup. They had come with another guide from the next station.

It had been dark for more than an hour when one of the three guides moved to the centre of the room and indicated that he was ready to go; he waved his right arm and said, 'Off.' On his head he had a woollen hat pulled well down over his ears, he wore a heavy woollen jacket, rope soled shoes and a pack on his back. The six of us and one other got up and followed him out of the door. As soon as he saw we were all there off he set, walking at a reasonable pace which we realised very quickly was a challenge to us to keep in contact with the person in front. Guides, we had been warned, kept going and were very disinclined to stop for anyone who could not keep pace. The first half of the night we walked up through the foothills, climbing most of the way. The trees got smaller and scantier until the path broke out into open rocky country with heather and boulders and streams racing down to the valley.

No one spoke as the going became more difficult, the pace never lessening. The path got lost in areas of limestone and shale. In the moonlight there were glimpses of mountain peaks projecting beyond the clouds and further up we came to snow.

Puffing and blowing the team kept up but it needed great concentration and determination not only to see where to go but to keep contact with the person in front. Walking at times became a scramble. After four hours, to our relief, the guide sat down and told us that there was a rest of ten minutes.

We lay down, exhausted, wondering how to cope with worse to come.

The guide got up and pulled in his belt, warning us that it was time to go. He said that we should now walk for another three hours and then rest for the morning. A minute later we were off again at the same pace through deeper snow which added to our difficulties.

At a point where the party was walking along an edge of snow-covered rock Helmut slipped and slithered down about ten feet. He yelled and the guide stopped momentarily until we had helped him back into line.

We were now quite high and there were the earliest signs of dawn away over the Mediterranean. This was a cheering sight which seemed to justify a little our general exhaustion and aching limbs. Louis had been right in advising me to exercise my legs for the climb in the mountains. Putting one leg in front of the other was no longer automatic, it had become a feat of will. Miles and miles of mountain peaks became visible as the light strengthened and the view over the sea was a welcome compensation. The upgrade flattened out and became a track which negotiated round the bases of the peaks and down into and across valleys. By nine o'clock, after eleven hours of walking and scrambling, our guide waved his arms at us and said, 'Stop here.'

He selected a recess in a rock face, sheltered from the wind, where there was a natural ledge in a niche in which to sit. I noticed that he had a revolver on his belt and sat in a position where he could view us all, now lying prostrate. He was in all respects in a commanding position and enjoyed it that way. If his followers were not exhausted he would have felt unrewarded.

'You will live,' Juan said, with a pitiless smile. 'Tonight will be downhill.'

Before long we had recovered sufficiently to gather round him and listen and try to understand his Spanish.

The plan was to leave here about midday. We were now on the border at the highest point where we crossed and this afternoon would walk the valleys and ridges of the upper plateau and then when it became dark descend into Spain. There were three hours in which to do nothing but eat our lunch and relax.

By three in the afternoon we were well into Spain and came to a large valley to cross. Juan suddenly stopped, there on the top of the other side were four men, obviously a frontier patrol. Juan pointed them out and indicated that we should have to change our course and cross the valley higher up. Two shots rang out across the valley. There was no obvious reason for this shooting coming from over a kilometre away but it was possibly to warn Juan to keep clear. By the time we had descended the valley and climbed the other side it was nearly dark and we saw nothing more of the patrol.

Climbing over the next ridge the lights of Spain became a revelation. Nearly three years of black-out had become a natural phenomenon. It was an exciting ghost of peace.

By ten o'clock at night, after almost continuous walking and trudging down the foothills and across the farmland we came within sight of the lights of a railway line. This, Juan told us, was our destination. In a field a half kilometre away was a pond with rushes. Here in a group we hid behind them with Juan at the side on the look out. Interminably we sat there waiting. For what was not obvious, but Juan stood alone and alert, watching for something. Suddenly we knew. Two flashes of a torch came from the station. It was our cue and Juan led us on in file to the little station where we were received by an official who ushered us all into a shed on the platform which would seem normally to have been a goods and luggage store. Generously the management provided a large wineskin of red wine to keep us contented through the night. Sufficient space on the floor was all that was needed. We had had no sleep since Toulouse.

Just after dawn a train came in. We were each given a ticket and put into a compartment. Seven of us sat together in an open longitudinal coach all looking bedraggled and filthy, unshaven with mud on our clothes, and there was nothing to do but wonder what could be our fate. It was noticeable that just before the train started a *Guardia civil* with a gun came to sit either side of us. When the control walked down the coach he looked at our tickets but asked for no papers. After a few friendly words with one of our guards he passed on. I remember wondering then what that little trip to Barcelona for the seven of us had cost and who had paid for it.

At Barcelona we went various ways. Helmut and I, for some reason, were met and conducted to a car by a man called Haddock. It turned out that he was the Consul's chauffeur, and after calling at the Consulate we were taken to his house. He had a charming wife and two children but very little food. Spain was then as short or even worse off than Occupied France. We lived practically on oranges, eating skin, pips and all. There was a little fish but no meat and a very meagre ration of bread and vegetables. Eating anything, with the family there, was embarrassing.

The diplomatic bag travelled each week by car to Madrid and we were very relieved and delighted to be told that the next trip would include us. In three days we were off. The Consul and his wife, Sir Harold and Lady Farquhar, were driven by Haddock in the first car and in the second were the carrier of the bag, another chauffeur and Helmut and myself.

We were well into the centre of Madrid when the two cars stopped at a large gate. The chauffeur spoke to the porter and showed him something out of his pocket. Then he drove into the grounds of a large house.

'This is the British Embassy. You are now on British soil and can relax,' said our friend with the bag.

Some time later a young lady came to greet us and apologised that we had been left alone. She was thirtyish with rolled up hair and a very happy smile and soon had us feeling that we were welcome.

'My name is Monica', said she, 'and I am secretary, receptionist, caterer and among other things it is my pleasant duty to look after you. Where have you come from?'

'Recently from Toulouse. This is Helmut, he is from Rotterdam, and I was Henri, a Frenchman until now but will revert to being British – my name is Philip.'

'Well done,' she said, and we completed the introduction by shaking hands. 'You will live here in the basement but can go out into the grounds. Don't go through the gate. It will be boring here, not going to see the City, but God forbid that you should land up in Miranda de Ebro!'

'I told him about Miranda,' chimed in Helmut; 'they warned me about that place when I was in Switzerland.'

Monica looked at us pitifully. 'So you see you will have to make your fun here with the girls in the basement. We are pretty used to entertaining all types.' She laughed and waved her hand towards the kitchen and told us that the ladies there were very affable and gastronomically minded.

We each had a room with a bed and chair and there was a large communal room with easy chairs and a dining table one end.

'There are only you two at the moment but two more of your party should join us tomorrow.'

'How long do we stay here?' I asked.

Monica thought for a moment. 'It varies quite a lot and depends on factors which I don't know about, but one day a bus will arrive and take you all away.'

'Where to?'

'I'm not sure about that either,' she added. 'Maybe Gibraltar.'

'Is it possible to send a message home to let my parents know?'

'Yes, that will be done through the War Office. Please write down the name and address of your nearest relative and I will see to it,' concluded Monica.

The next morning I was warned to be ready to meet the Ambassador, Sir Samuel Hoare. Lady Hoare had already been to visit us in the basement and brought us some recent books and papers.

Sir Samuel was very keen to pump me on conditions in the camps and to know if we were getting sufficiently overfed to make up for any deficiencies. He explained how short food was in Spain. A bakery had been built in the grounds and imported flour from Gibraltar assured a ready supply of white bread for all who worked in the Embassy.

He had heard of the expected arrival of two British officers that evening, coming from Switzerland, but had no idea of their names or unit. He suggested that we put up two more beds for them.

That afternoon two more of our own party arrived and in the evening the two British officers were driven in. To my amazement one was Airey Neave, who a year previously had been a fellow inmate in Oflag IX A/H at Spangenberg, and the other was Hugh Woollatt. Airey had escaped from Oflag IVC at Colditz and Hugh from Stalag VB at Biberach.

They had come through the Nouveaus' flat and by the same route over the Pyrenees.

Unknown to us then we were parcels of the PAT line named after its chief, Patrick Albert O'Leary. Formerly he had been a doctor in the Belgian army but later escaped to Britain and became an officer in the Royal Navy where he had assumed this clandestine name. His real name was Albert-Marie Guérisse. Later he was captured in a small boat when attempting to rescue Polish airmen from the French coast just north of the Spanish border. He got out of gaol and was personally responsible for the creation of an escape line which rallied in Marseille and passed over the eastern Pyrenees. Eventually he was betrayed to the Gestapo in March 1943, and after more than two years of unmitigated hell was liberated from Dachau in April 1945.

Among over twenty awards from various countries he holds the George Cross and Distinguished Service Order from Britain.

Ever since Marcelle had stepped delicately into my life and I had clicked with Mario, who had led me to the welcome efficiency and warmth of the Nouveaus' flat, I had marvelled at my luck and wondered who was the genius and from whence had come the intuition and the motivating force.

That evening the Ambassador and Lady Hoare and the Staff of the Embassy gave a party in which sherry flowed in ample measure and the ladies in the kitchen were overjoyed to show us what could be achieved in a starving country. It was not until late in the evening that the news of our departure the next morning, a little secret from Monica, was allowed to filter out.

When the Senior Staff tactfully withdrew the celebration matured to a more intimate level and it was well past midnight when we crept into bed.

There was no hitch about our departure. Soon after breakfast a bus arrived, there was a driver and three others inside. The six of us bundled our way in and soon learned that they had left Miranda at six that morning. Quite a number gathered round to give us an emotional send off. Monica had told us that we should be in Gibraltar by the following evening. Off we went, with the girls waving and blowing kisses but no sign of a senior member of the staff. Officially it was an event which never happened.

Fifty kilometres outside Madrid we were stopped by a couple of *carabineras*. It seemed a mutually accepted procedure. The two, who had been sitting by the roadside, got up when they saw the bus and stood in the middle of the road. They chatted with the driver in a friendly manner and he showed some papers, sticking up nine digits and swinging his arm around towards us. Heads nodded, then out got the driver and opened up the two back doors. Here, on the back seat, were stacked white loaves and tins of bully beef. A loaf and a tin were given to each and that seemed to be the pass to proceed. Exactly the same sort of thing happened at varying intervals. It was always a tin and a loaf each and mutual understanding never appeared to be in doubt. The driver, a little man in a peaked cap and with a red comic face, was delighted with his priceless load and we soon got to waving and cheering each pair as we were released to go on our way.

By the evening we had got into the mountains and spent the night in a hotel in Cordoba. We slept and ate in a separate part and were not allowed to converse with the other guests or go outside into the town. We talked and drank late into the night as a sort of dress rehearsal for the celebration to come in Gibraltar.

Secretly perhaps, we assumed that news would have got there before us, that the flags would be up and a welcome arranged for the occasion. How wrong we were.

The bus left the next morning with its chosen nine holding their heads in response to an indulgent night but sustained by thoughts of even better things to come.

Penetrating the mountains we broke through to the coast at Malaga, and there our driver, realising that a 'hair of the hound' would be nectar to help us for the rest of the way, stopped at a restaurant and apart from providing a lot of local wine and other forms of sustenance was seen to foot the bill. The journey along the coastal road was hot and soporific and eventually we could see the dark mass of the Rock before we came to the frontier at La Linea. Here there was no sign of bustle. An official or two came and looked at us and showed little interest.

There was a wait for over an hour while those on the other side of the line decided to accept us. It happened to be Saturday afternoon as it was surreptitiously pointed out when we got to the Guard Room. No one suggested that escape parties would be far more welcome on a weekday but there was some indication to assume such a solution.

It was clear that anyone arriving from Spain should be treated with suspicion. Neave, Woollatt and I were creamed off as officers and put under guard in a separate room. It took another four hours for Intelligence to be satisfied that nothing hostile had been swallowed.

Then we were free and were taken down through the town for an evening out. The streets were bursting with service men of all sorts. It was said that there were fifteen thousand on the Rock and among them a handful of Wrens. What a time they had. Our companion had chosen the yacht club as a suitable place for supper but he had not found out that a few Wrens were there and the world had come to see what a British girl looked like. One of them sat on the counter with fifty men drinking around her, an emblem of the absent sex.

She was well poised, her hat at a chosen angle, her skirt a little above her knees and with an expression of responsive warmth, but oblivious it appeared of being very definitely the centre of appeal.

The idea caught on that we had just come out of Germany and had had no opportunity as yet to celebrate. Both elements were an ample excuse for a party and the spirit took over.

I do not remember leaving the Yacht Club but woke some hours later in the RAMC Headquarters with a head the worse for wear.

Gibraltar was a hive of many enterprises. It was the nucleus of naval, military and airforce activities for a large area.

To make the runway suitable for larger aircraft it was being extended into the sea. Lorries full of rock raced outwards along the rough tracks to the dumping spots and returned empty, for more, at great speed. At the same time more space within the Rock was needed and noise from blasting was accepted as inevitable. I joined a party headed by Lord Gort and the Senior Medical Officer to inspect the hospital in the rock which it was planned to enlarge. Safe as it may have been it was not the ideal place for convalescent relaxation.

During the few days that passed in Gibraltar, Neave, Woollatt and I became nuclei for those wishing to indulge and celebrate so that the time slipped into an alcoholic haze until we eventually found outselves on the boat for home. It was a troopship which made a wide detour out into the Atlantic before running in for Glasgow.

•

The weather in the Clyde on that morning, 13th May, had no element which could enhance any feeling of welcome we might have had on seeing our island, still the home of the free. Low cloud and mist hung around with little wind to blow it away.

Gourock, where we landed, was not any different. There were no families to greet the troops who had been abroad for long periods and there was a wait in the station for over an hour.

In Glasgow we arrived in a hotel and were told that we would remain there until the night train for London.

While everyone sat around I longed to phone home and decided that this was the moment but I had no cash. Just as a possible source was being worked out who should walk in but Airey's sister, Rosamund. She was there purely by chance and had no idea that Airey had come home. The last news their family had had was of his arrival in Switzerland. Rosamund was in Scotland on holiday. After all the greetings and explanations I asked her for a little money to phone.

It was a great moment as I waited, hearing the phone ringing and wondering if there would be anyone at home. There was. It was my mother.

'Oh, it's you, darling, how marvellous! I got a telegram to say you were coming home.'

A suspicion suddenly clicked – why I?

'Darling, your father died just before I got the telegram.'

Then there was silence and I could hear her crying and sniffing. Then my mother spoke again.

'He had been working far too hard. He came home with a terrible headache and was determined to go to Brixham. He became unconscious on Paddington Station and died in St Mary's Hospital. It was a cerebral haemorrhage.'

I stood there wrapped in depression. I had been very fond of my father, but had seen little of him since I had qualified as a doctor eight years ago. I remember having thought that I would be able to get to know him again during my leave.

Now it was all a passing dream. Mother would miss him desperately, they were a devoted couple.

I returned to the group, and they were very quick to realise that something was wrong. I told them of my great loss and sat down among them with nothing to say. They, particularly Airey and his sister and Hugh Woollatt, were all in a celebrating mood but I felt lost, with an intense desire to get home as soon as possible.

There were two alternatives, to leave them and go off for a long walk and let them get on with it or to stay and celebrate gastronomically and try to rejoice in the obvious fact that we were home.

A Military Police sergeant appeared and asked for me by name. His hat was slightly back and he had a large moustache. 'Is there a Major Newman here?' Various indications transferred the conversation to me. 'Where are you from, Sir?'

'I have come from Gibraltar. Before that I was a prisoner of war. There are two other officers here,' and I introduced them.

'Where do we go from here?' I asked.

'You will go to Euston on the evening train. I will contact you later with temporary passes so please stay here where I can find you.'

In the evening the sergeant took us to the platform, having issued us all with passes. There was a corporal, who had come from Germany, with no pass and a scene arose at the barrier. The Military Police refused to let him get on the train. We were adamant that he should go, but an officer who had appeared at the last moment said that he would have to wait until the next day.

Airey Neave, in very strong language, told the officer what he thought of the arrangements. Then the whistle blew. The three of us pushed through the barrier, taking the corporal with us and got him on to the train.

Early next morning we arrived at Euston and the three of us were taken to the hotel for breakfast. Here we were in London but by no means free to go. The Military Police were there to see that we got to the right place. Leave was a far thought; in fact it was three weeks before I was released from interrogation in different departments, all asking much the same questions.

After breakfast we were taken to Marylebone Station, to the Great Central Hotel, which was our first contact with Military Intelligence. An orderly took me to the first floor, sat me down and produced the inevitable form to fill in. There was a wait and then I was ushered into the presence of an interrogating officer. Initially he had my interest but after preliminary chat it became obvious that he was not really curious and his questions were pedestrian and could have been put to any of my colleagues. He was not at all interested to know how I got out of the camp or into Spain.

I got to Liverpool Street and found a train for Ingatestone. To my joy I found Airey and Rosamund already there. He had become disenchanted by his interview and decided to plead for release.

When we arrived at the little station there were my mother and Airey's father. We hugged and kissed.

Behind us stood the Station Master, watching the touching

scene. As we left all four of us stopped and greeted him and shook hands very warmly.

'Why are they letting all these people out of Germany?' he said.

Neither of us replied.

Index

Index